–THE–
Italian
RECKONING

MARK TORO

authorHOUSE

AuthorHouse™
1663 Liberty Drive
Bloomington, IN 47403
www.authorhouse.com
Phone: 833-262-8899

Published by AuthorHouse 07/22/2022

ISBN: 978-1-6655-5783-2 (sc)
ISBN: 978-1-6655-6282-9 (hc)
ISBN: 978-1-6655-5782-5 (e)

Print information available on the last page.

This is a novel based on true events. Names have changed and any resemblance to
actual persons, living or dead, are entirely coincidental.

This book is printed on acid-free paper.

Dedication and Gratitude

To Michael Del Percio, my dear uncle friend, (and wife Cora), thank you for your belief in me, your interest in my writing of books and my photography, your mentorship for my kitchen design career and your sincere friendship. I will miss you.

For Mrs. Diana Maselli, the dear English teacher, from Niles McKinley High School, who first taught me the value of reading, then many years later, watched me read from my first novel. She inspired me to continue, by saying, "Keep dreaming and chasing those dreams."
I forever thank you.

For Dick Cretcher, my teacher and mentor, from Ohio Institute of Photography, who always gave me sound fatherly advice, and numerous letters of recommendation when I needed them. Your belief in me, allowed me to continue to grow in my art and profession. Wherever my career went, you were always there.
I forever thank you.

For Tony Napolet, the high school football coach and caring teacher, who saw that I was set on the right track early on, when teenage life was difficult. You got me back to church, got me into karate, gave me a workout dummy and let me take my driver's test with your family car.
I'll never forget the positive influence you had on my life.
I forever thank you.

With Thanks

Thank you to those who have expressed continual support and interest in this novel, you are: Bruce Maggiano, Tim Buchman, Dick and Dorothy Cretcher, Nancy Carbone, Dante Holland, Ron Haynie, Mike Lehner and countless others not mentioned.

To brother Lance, thank you for your support of me and my story. It has meant a great deal. To brother Greg, thank you for the sharing of all the music, and for allowing me to tag along to all those shows. To brother Dana, thank you for all the years you spent taking care of our dear mom, when the rest of us were not able to. I know it helped prolong her years. To brother Alfonso, III, Love, Hope and Prayers for your life. There's always hope that we'll be reunited someday. Love to all my brothers.

To my Mom, Mary Lou, who taught me to never give up, for our pivotal rescue and for our family's love and strength. You raised five boys alone, and juggled it all. I am so grateful for what you taught me. To my grandfather, William "Bill" Sullivan, who selflessly provided us with a new loving home at a most critical time in our family's history. Love to you both.

To Roberto Marino, Thank you for the ancestry information on my grandfather Alfonso Toro, Sr. and grandmother Flora Yannucci Toro.

Extra special thanks to my dear friends, Tazio and Rossana Atriano, without whom, this story would not have been possible, as you both kindly welcomed me back to my love of Italy, with your warm hospitality and friendship.

The Train to Pescara

"Did this just happen?" I thought to myself, as I finished four days and nights, in the one place I always dreamed of going, Venice, Italy. I was on a bullet train on the way down the Adriatic coast to Pescara, my grandfather's hometown region. The train was second class, a necessary change, but still smooth and fast. It was June and I was taking stock of the last seven days, reviewing all the photographs I had made in hectic, magical wonder. This was the greatest photo assignment of my life, and I was the main client. It would take a bit of time for my heart and mind to catch up on all that I had captured and seen. It couldn't have happened more perfect, with only a few bumps in the road.

How blessed and lucky I was to have made my first trip to Italy, achieving what I did, only eight months before the most horrible modern day pandemic that would cripple Italy and the rest of the world, the Corona virus. With a vaccine rolling out, it's hard to say how many days we each have, as this virus appears to be taking people out at random. With life precious, it's more important than ever, to tell all that had happened, on the greatest experience of my life.

Before Venice, there had been Rome, a remarkable city, my first encounter with Italy, where every block was an outdoor museum, filled to the brim with history, the best art and architecture in the world and Bernini's statues, that seemed to be everywhere, which left an amazing impression on me. To get started, I needed to have my first real cup of espresso, and two blocks from my hotel, I had found just the place, that I would return to again and again. That first sip took me to java heaven, unlike any other time before.

After St. Peter's Basilica, The Sistine Chapel and The Colosseum, I spent extra time at The Pantheon, Rome's oldest building intact, a place that defies explanation. With its perfect unsupported dome, that could fit a perfectly round 142 foot diameter ball inside, and the hole in the roof, with view to the stars and sky, this had a huge impact on me, enough that I would have to visit it twice.

Rome set the stage for Venice, where I had left the historical and entered the magical. Spending an hour with The Bronze Horses on the roof of St. Mark's Basilica, in Piazza San Marco, I ended up making a top photograph. The next morning, floating on a gondola boat, under the Bridge of Sighs, through the quiet canals, past Marco Polo's house, I felt so fortunate to be alive. Was I dreaming? It felt like heaven. I had arrived.

Rome and Venice would lead to something greater, in a different way, and I was only a day away.

As I draw closer to my grandfather's hometown of Moscufo, Italy, in the Pescara region, I realize that touching his hometown is just as much about reconnecting to my past with my grandfather, and the few memories I have about him, but more so about reconnecting to my heritage and the loss of my Italian father, Alonso Jr.

Will there be something waiting for me in Pescara, or even Moscufo, where my father's father had lived before he came to America in 1911 at age sixteen?

As I approach Pescara, after a glorious time in Rome and Venice, I feel they are with me; my father, Alonso, Jr., my grandmother Gia and my grandfather, Alonso, Sr.

What was so pivotal for my spirit, my soul, to be moved enough to make the greatest trip of my life, and to make it all alone? The photographs I wanted to make was the number one reason for crossing the Atlantic to Italy, for this boy so romantic. Was there another reason that I had yet to discover?

It's interesting how, when I landed in Venice, that the first matter at hand was changing the two train route, leaving Venice to Pescara, to one train. I didn't want to miss a connecting train, with so little time in between. I had discovered through a photographer friend Ted, from the photo school, Ohio Institute of Photography, we had attended years ago, that there was a single train route. Ted had given me helpful tips for navigating the land, for as a photographer himself, he had traveled to Italy a dozen or so times. Little did I realize, that this train change would allow me to arrive five hours early to Pescara, giving me an extra cushion of time of two full days there. This would allow me to take a bus or taxi to Moscufo on the second day.

Even though I would lose my first class status on this single train, the train clerk told me, "I'll put you in the middle of the car near all the luggage. You'll be fine." I had heard a few bad stories of luggage being stolen off trains between stops.

Immediately after checking in at The Best Western Hotel Plaza, at the Piazza Sacro Cuore Square in Pescara, the hotel clerk had been overly helpful in getting me the bus schedule after I asked, "Is there a bus that goes to Moscufo?" Right underneath the counter, he brought the schedule up, as if from a magician's hat. Suddenly, It was all laid out for me how I would get there. On that second day in Pescara, I would take the bus to Moscufo, from Pescara Centrale, arriving at 10:17 a.m., being dropped off at the center of this small commune village, right near the town's piazza, the Piazza Umberto in Moscufo.

However, I'm getting way too ahead of myself. To understand how the events led up to all of this, we need to go back, long before I started to plan my trip.

A Tailor's Invitation

There was a reason Italy picked me…
to go across the sea.

I had mixed emotions about taking my first trip to Italy. This went way back to my youth. It took years, decades even, to reach the peace that enabled me to even want to go and be part of it. Part of wanting to be Italian again. After all this time, I more than earned it.

Excitement ran through me, months before. "I'm really going!" I kept telling myself, after the trip was booked in advance. Now, I was ready to go. I used to say all the time, "Will I ever make it to Italy?"

One day, seven years earlier, I met Tonio at the big box home improvement store where I worked. I'll never forget the look on his face, when I pinned him as an old timer from Italy, with a strangely, familiar accent, and I mentioned that my grandfather had come from Moscufo by Pescara.

The older Italian man exclaimed with wide eyes, "Me too! I'm from Moscufo!"

"No Way! No Sir!" I said.

"This is interesting!" I thought to myself. I had never met another person directly from my grandfather's hometown before, since I was an adult, and from over thirty years living in Columbus, Ohio. "This is a unique thing," I thought, as I showed him around the appliance showroom. That chance meeting turned into beautiful friendship, with this uncle-like friend. That started everything for me to really want to go to Italy. Because now, this chance encounter had turned into a positive force from the land of my ancestors. My relationship to Italy was changing overnight.

Shortly after, Tonio invited me into his home, where I was met and welcomed by his sweet wife Rosa. It was as if I had known them my whole life, as I kissed his wife on the cheek like an aunt of long ago, like all us Italians do when we greet each other. That was the warmth we had between us from the beginning. My first visit, Rosa served in great Italian style, the small cup of liquor and a slice of orange cake.

That night, in their home, Tonio showed me a book on Moscufo, and tales of living there. The town both he and my grandfather had come from. Then, he gave me a brochure from Moscufo. It featured the details of a beautiful historic landmark church from the fourteenth century, called Santa Maria del Lago, of Romanesque architecture. If I ever made it there, it would be high on the list to visit. This church was the centerpiece of the town.

Tonio continued to tell me about life in this town, and I couldn't help but think that this was a peculiar moment, but so wonderful, that here was a guy I had just met, from my grandfathers hometown in Italy, and he had invited me to his home, where he and his wife are being so beautifully gracious to me, and I'm given a token from a place of my forefathers. Looking back, that brochure from Moscufo, was my invitation to Italy, from a man I had just met on my job, who's now telling me what it was like in Moscufo, from pictures in a book and stories from his life.

That night, a fiery, passionate interest took hold inside of me, and suddenly I wanted to get to Italy. But how? I had no idea how I would ever afford getting there, but now, I had a connection to that land, and *I had to get there.* I had unofficially been invited.

I began to see Tonio and Rosa now and then in the big box home improvement store where I worked, and the grocery store. Every time it was a joy to see them, with warm embraces and kisses, just like it was years ago with my aunts and uncles, when we walked through the back door at my grandma and grandpa's home, back in my hometown of Warren, Ohio, a neighboring city of Youngstown. I didn't know it at the time, but these new Italian friends of mine, were plucked just for me. There was a big reason they came into my life. They were introducing me back to all things Italy, on what had been severed years ago. They were also restoring my faith in Italian folk in general, that too had been severed.

Tonio mentioned how he visited Moscufo about every two years and how he spoke to his friends there about every month. His friends would tell him how he was crazy for still working full time at age 78, but Tonio would tell me how when he visited, his friends would just sit around and do nothing and many had died off. "Who's the crazy one, eh?" He would tell me laughing.

He worked as a tailor, like his father before him, who had been trained in Rome, and Tonio had been the top tailor in Columbus for more than thirty years. When he had retired his business years ago, a top client of his asked him to become his personal tailor, so Tonio continued to work well into his eighties for this one family. He was given an offer he couldn't refuse.

It's worthy to note, that before meeting Tonio, I was put in touch with my older brother Gavino's cousin-in-law, Riccardo from Cleveland, whose family also had come from Moscufo. Riccardo had sent me my grandfather's ship's manifest from 1911 and birth certificate, dated 1895. When I told him I had met Tonio from Moscufo, he said, "That guy made my father's wedding suit in Italy some fifty years ago. I came to Columbus to see him with my father when I was a kid."

So, before I made my trip to Italy, I met these two people, rooted from Moscufo, who knew each other, and I became connected in the middle. Two layers of connection to my grandfathers's hometown now touched my life before I even got there.

Something was being laid out.

I hadn't even begun to realize how much.

Flight 333

I had met Caroline, the travel lady, back in October of 2018 and finally decided, "I must do this. Tomorrow is not promised." I had enough in my 401K to take the dive and realized, if I didn't do this now, the opportunity may never come again.

She organized a ten day trip with a few half day guided tours in Rome and Venice to cover the top spots. I got the trip organized to where it would be a good introduction to Italy. I decided against hop, skip and jump approach over more cities on a tour bus, where you never really get to see any depth in any one place. So, I decided on three places, four tops. The following year, it was all set for a shove off by the end of May. I put my money down that locked in the package. Soon after, I injured my knee in a bad way.

It would be a few months before I could get an MRI, to see how bad it was. Then, it was confirmed that I had a meniscus tear in my right knee and I would need surgery. Because of all this, my trip was temporarily put on hold. Knee surgery was done Mid-February, and all went well. Physical therapy got my knee strengthened and healing was on schedule. Italy was back on, and now a few months later, I was gearing up with preparation for a big trip. The biggest trip of my life.

It became real and after years of dreaming it, I was finally going to Italy. It hadn't sunk in until the day I was getting on the plane.

I was a bit anxious about flying across the Atlantic for the first time and we would be in the air for over nine hours. To let you know how God put me at ease about the flight, I got the "333" on my phone before boarding, as it was the flight number from Charlotte-to-Rome. I chuckled when the number came up, as the number 333 had come to be known as "Comfort, God's Presence" to me. Others call it the Angel number.

Believe what you will, but…

To give you some history on the 333 and what it has meant for me, it started around eight years ago, when I started seeing it regularly. I would be needing God's reassurance at times because of the difficult period I was going through, post divorce, and looking up, I would just happen to see the 333 on my car clock. Then, the 333 on the time clock at work, the stove clock at home, the gas station price sign and on my watch. It would be the context of the situation on where, when and how I would see it. I would just happen to glance up and there it was, ready for me to see, in my sightline, at that particular moment.

Quite possibly, God could have done all those 333's previously, getting me ready to be reassured with my flight to Italy, years later. The 333 meant for me more specifically, God The Father, The Lord Jesus Christ and The Holy Spirit. It represented The Holy Trinity. The 333 was the Trinity.

So, when I got the flight details and saw the 333 on my phone as the flight number from Charlotte to Rome, I chuckled like I always do. This time, it calmed my fears about flying that far, because in essence, God was on board and in the midst of my Italy trip plans, watching over me. After seeing that, I was no longer worried. He chose to tell me in that specific way. He was blessing the trip before I even got off the ground.

It was a signpost for me, God's way of saying, "I understand and care what concerns you. I'm here." The 333 came to show that it was not some coincidence I was looking for. So, for the doubters, it was God's real presence manifested physically for me to see.

Race to Bernini's

Flying across The Atlantic Ocean, I was amazed I was finally on my way. That a plane could even fly that far, was totally new for me to experience. The jet had real time google maps displayed in front of me, showing progress of the flight. Speed, altitude, distance yet to Rome, temperature. As we got close, flying over France, seeing its mountains was striking. Then I saw it. My first view of Italy. The Italian coast. Seeing that for the first time touched my heart so deep. "Oh my gosh! There it is! There's Italy! My dream! I'm almost there,"I thought to myself. "This is unreal!"

We were shuttled from the airport and after I checked in, I was starting to gear up for photo shoot mode. I was so excited but anxious to start. This was my life's greatest photo assignment about to begin. My trip was now all about making the photographs.

Taking on a trip of this magnitude, I had some reservations, and some fears, because I had chosen to travel to Italy alone. The reason being, that I knew if I were to travel with someone on my first trip, I would not be able to go wherever I wanted, for the photographs I needed to make.

My biggest fear was that I would have an overwhelming sense of loneliness. But, as soon as I landed in Rome, got settled a bit, then hit the streets with my camera, those fears melted

First View of the Italian Coast

away. It was my time alone in the land of my dreams, the foreign land of my heart. Instead of loneliness, I felt a great peace, because my traveling was in line with my purpose of a solo trip, for reasons I didn't fully understand yet.

One, I had made it to Italy. Two, I was energized and fully engaged for the photographs I was there to make, that caused great excitement. Three, God was with me, and He made me feel that, by how smooth everything went for the whole ten days, not counting surprises that would unfold for me later. Four, I had the greatest new camera gear I couldn't wait to use.

I had a feeling that my life would be forever changed prior to this trip. Like everything before was "Pre-Italy" and everything after was "Post-Italy," divided by a distinct line. This trip was a necessary part of my evolution.

The Travelgrams Tour shuttle driver I found holding a sign, near the front door, after I made my way through the crowd, with my two rolling suitcases at the Leonardo da Vinci-Fiumicino Airport in Rome. We exchanged pleasantries, as he said, "Hi." Ok, this way please." We walked to a van parked out front and we got in and quickly drove away through the congested streets of Rome. This could have been some stranger driving me to some remote far off place, but I felt assured and at ease. I thought this was fairly personalized, as he was there to pick up just me.

Now, it was real. I'm in Rome on my way to the hotel. "Oh Wow!" I said to myself, looking at everything outside the windows. I was fascinated by everything.

We drove through a maze of streets in thick traffic, and seeing his GPS on his dash, I saw that we were only minutes away from the hotel in the Prati District. I took a few snaps out the window on the way. Even ordinary scenes out the window in Rome were extraordinary. Suddenly we stopped and we were at the hotel. It had only been a twenty minute ride. It was only 11:55 a.m., but six hours ahead of US time, so I had a long day ahead of me. I felt pretty good for having only four hours sleep on a choppy night flight.

Before getting inside the hotel, I tipped the driver a ten Euro for getting me there in good shape and in reasonable time. Next, was meeting my Travelgrams Tour Host, in which there were two, but the one due there now had stepped out and was due back anytime, so they put my luggage in a holding room, while I waited in the hotel lobby. The host would check me into the hotel, give me maps, itinerary and tips on what was nearby in the immediate area.

I was in Rome, Italy. The hotel was quiet and empty and I was anxious to get going into the streets with my camera, but I had to wait until I got connected with my host who had all the essential information, but first get me checked in.

She appeared about twenty minutes later, and the hotel clerk motioned me to her, and she came over to meet me.

"Hi, I'm Anna. You are on the tour, Yes?" She asked.

"Yes, I'm Marco Conte," I replied.

"I'll give you some information in a few minutes," and we walked over to some tables that were there for everyone that had the tour package.

She looked at the list and found me. "You are on for Vatican Tour tomorrow, St. Peter's and Colosseum. Tomorrow buffet breakfast opens at 7:00 a.m and we meet here at 7:30 a.m. Be sure to not be late or they leave without you."

"How far are we from St. Peter's?" I asked. "I heard it's close."

"Oh, Yes, very close. Ten minutes away."

"Oh my gosh," I thought. "Ten minutes away? St. Peter's?" I had just got to Italy and it had not sunk in yet. She gave me some materials and we walked over to the front desk and I was checked in.

I thanked her, and got my luggage, and now I was on my own. I took the elevator up and got settled into my room, freshened up and checked out all my photo gear. I noticed every time I took the elevator up and down, that the wall paper surrounding the elevator door had a large, blown up photograph of The Trevi Fountain. It was both cheesy and cool.

I had brought two photo bags and did much research on their size and function. A larger bag for traveling on the plane and trains. A smaller bag for my treks into the cities, museums and tour sites, as there were size restrictions for these important sites. I didn't want to get stuck checking a bag with an expensive camera.

It was great, new gear. A newer generation Sony mirrorless camera I had bought earlier in the year, and some new lenses. I also had a back up cell phone camera with a 64 GB memory card. The Sony Alpha 6300 was next generation of the ever popular A6000 I had purchased in 2016. Only the A6300 was improved upon with better quality sensor, higher resolution electronic viewfinder, a magnesium alloy body, slightly thicker. It was a phenomenal camera along with three lenses, and had all the capability I would ever need; an inspiration in itself. It was compact but had the weight and substance I needed. This trip would put the new gear through its greatest tests.

I switched over all my gear, camera, lenses, memory cards, chargers, etc., into my smaller camera bag that was perfect size that would not draw too much attention, for all my treks out in the street, so I could move around easily.

I had mapped out in advance, all the key areas of Rome for my limited three days there. This was aided by a photography school friend I had reconnected with, just months after planning my trip. Ted had been to Italy a dozen or so times, over the years, and photographed it up and down, so his help in navigating was greatly instrumental. This was not without my own study with the many books I had digested on Rome and Venice before I left. But, I wouldn't know how it would really play out until I got a feel for the place, touched ground and got out and got going. Then, instinct took over on how I needed to work it, on how much time was needed in each place, how to pace myself and the light at a given time of day.

I needed lunch and two blocks away I found a great cafe where I had my first, real espresso, which was like a bomb of concentrated coffee flavor, the opposite of Russian vodka, but almost gave the same reaction. On the other end of the cafe, was their pizza, that they would cut with scissors into 4x6" squares and serve on a breadboard. In between was a twenty-five foot long desert bar. I had my three slices, waited for a bit, taking in all the bustling activity, but then I needed to get moving. I had to get those first photos behind me, then I'd feel on the mark.

My hotel was close to St. Peter's Square and Castel Sant'Angelo, on Via Virgilio, in the Prati District. After I had my lunch, I started walking back past the hotel and toward Castel Sant'Angelo (The Castle of The Holy Angel). I couldn't wait to see Bernini's Angels that lined the Bridge of Angels corridor leading up to this monument that had so much history. That was the common thread throughout Rome. Everything had an immense amount of history.

It was only a few blocks from the hotel to the Park Adriano, a garden type square on the way, that was filled with iconic umbrella pines. Then, I could see the round building in the distance, only a few blocks away. Walking down the corridor with the angel statues by Bernini on both sides, it hit me that I was in a most, special place. I was on the Bridge of Angels. Minutes later, I began to make my first photographs. The late afternoon sun started piercing through the overcast clouds, after I had been shooting for half an hour. Now, the definition details of the angels came alive with the sun's illumination.

I pondered for a few minutes, as I stood on the bridge amongst the clusters of people flowing past me, taking it all in, and I thought, "This is too much. This is where "Angels and Demons" was filmed. Bernini's Angels. Oh Gosh! These are breathtaking. That man sculpted those. I can't believe I'm here. I just flew thousands of miles over the ocean to get here, only a few hours ago. Now, I'm here with my camera. "Oh God, Thank you so much for getting me here."

I stood in the corridor with Bernini's angels on both sides, ten angels in all. This was my first encounter with Italy, and my eyes welled up. Tears were ready to drop. Then, I realized I had limited time, limited minutes, for everything I would see.

"Photos to make Marco," I told myself. "Right." Then, I sprung into action and started analyzing the scene. "What's the best way to photograph these angels, this place?" I thought to myself. I moved up and down the corridor, changing lenses for the best viewpoint, the best compression of background for the angels. A short while later, the sun popped out again from the flat day, God blessing the scene, for me to get the best out of it. Now it was looking good. Lighting is everything.

The afternoon sun defined the detail on Bernini's Angels. Their form came alive. I kept zeroing in, moving, adjusting distance, adjusting zoom, adjusting composition. Those angels

Castel Sant'Angelo, Angel with Spear, Rome

Castel Sant'Angelo, Angel with Column

looked real, frozen in time. After some test shots behind me, I was getting warmed up, feeling my stride. It's all I needed to get started.

With a mental inventory of all I had photographed, and reviewing my digital camera screen, I checked to see if I had missed anything. I worked the scene for forty-five minutes and was fairly comfortable on what I had captured. It was time to move on. Many times, I always work a scene until finished, until I have exhausted all possibilities.

After Castel Sant'Angelo, I began walking toward St. Peter's Square, feeling my way down the narrow streets. Scooters zoomed by it seemed like every five minutes, the preferred method of transportation in Rome. I had challenges for the rest of the day and had to keep moving. I was on four hours sleep after flying for ten hours.

As I walked a block away, turning around, I framed the round building between the narrow street. Then, I moved on. "St. Peter's is next. We'll see how that goes. I can't believe I'm on my way there. This is really something," I thought.

That first engagement with Rome, out with my camera, was so surreal. As I was walking, I thought, "It's a miracle I'm here. I need to get my photos and touch the land."

There was something else in the air that I felt. I couldn't place it. God saw fit that I had finally made it. Something was in the background. A hidden mystery. I had no idea how much this little mystery would have my trip take a left turn, down the road a bit. But, there were photos to make, and all I knew were my daily photo goals at hand, my half day photo goals. As long as I held to that, I had a good chance of capturing all that my heart desired for the places I had time to see.

Whatever that something else in the air was, that mystery hadn't sunk in yet. It could have been that my senses were on overload, a Stendahl effect, on all I was taking in, or lack of sleep. But no, my intuition was telling me that it was something I would have to eventually pay attention to, but that something would have to wait. There were too many photos to make. It was the main priority over everything else, and to get a feel for the place.

Before assignments, like in any of the important photo shoots of the past, I would always write down a "Shot List." There would be key photos that I had to get. Bucket list photos. After finishing my shots at Castle Sant'Angelo, my first location, I was happy and glad to have that under my belt. That mini-success would set the stage for all the rest in Rome.

A few blocks and traffic lights later, I walked down Via della Conciliazione and into St. Peter's Square, which was inside the border of Vatican City, the smallest country in the world. After I crossed the border, I got my first photograph, as the setting sun glistened off the old bricks that made up the ground, while admiring St. Peters dome, designed by Michelangelo. So much history surrounded me here. This was where St. Peter, Christ's apostle, began his church.

The light was spectacular, as late afternoon sun played off the curvature of the surrounding arc of the buildings that bordered the inside of the square, with the roof edge lined with statues of the saints. The fountain sprayed on the left side, and the obelisk pillar stood in the middle, the site where St. Peter was crucified upside down. How many people visit this site and don't understand what really happened here?

After I got all my introductory shots of St. Peter's Square, and the sun was dipping low, I had to think about getting back

St. Peter's Square, First Day in Rome.

to the hotel before dark. I was alone and had only a rough idea of the terrain. I walked away down Via della Conciliazione, the main corridor that connects St. Peter's to Castel Sant'Angelo. As I turned around, it was another gorgeous picture waiting for me to snap, with St. Peter's dome silhouetted between rows of buildings highlighted by golden setting sun. I waited for the right amount of people to walk into the photograph.

Before I was out of the area, I noticed a gelato shop nearby, with people seated at small tables outside the doorway, enjoying this desert. I had to try it. I settled on pistachio and chocolate, one scoop each, the only flavors I would get for the rest of my trip. The contrasting flavors made it my favorite. An amazing style ice cream.

I took a close up photo of me holding the gelato cup with a spoon stuck in the untouched desert before it melted, and an out of focus St. Peter's dome in the distant background. That perfectly summed up the end of my first day in Rome. A treat and sights for the eyes, amazing delights under Italian skies.

I finished walking back to the NH Collection Giustiniano Hotel before nightfall. I had done good on my first day, getting warmed up with two major sites, plenty of photographs in color and black and white, and getting comfortable walking Rome by myself. 19,000 steps on four hours sleep, especially after the knee operation earlier in the year and having no residual pain. Not bad. It felt good getting all that under my belt in Rome on my first day.

Walking Away from St. Peter's on First Day

First Gelato in Rome

As I was eating a great plate of pasta, in the hotel restaurant, one of my best dinners on my whole trip, I felt a bit of sadness creep in, thinking about my Italian father and how he must be happy looking down, seeing me in Italy, a place he never got to see. The sadness would come and go, thinking about all those years lost without my father, but also, without our Italian family. The big question that followed me on the whole arc of my life was, "Why did it have to happen? How could an Italian family do that to five young boys who lost their father in their youth? Why had we been cut out of the picture, no longer belonging or included?"

Pantheon Effect

The second day in Rome, was the tour of The Vatican Museum, The Sistine Chapel, St. Peter's Basilica and The Colosseum. It was the tour I had signed up for, but after arriving, I had heard of another half-day tour I could add, "The Highlights of Rome Walking Tour." It would give me an introduction to the three sites I was planning on visiting on my third and last day, the Piazza Navona, The Pantheon and the Trevi Fountain.

"This is great!" I thought. The tour will show me these three places, the day before I planned to go, but with some history from our tour guide Falco, and I could return on my third and last day to revisit any of these three popular sites. Out of those three landmarks, The Pantheon gave me the most striking impression from all of Rome. There were the pillars at the entrance that were solid travertine stone, unlike the ones at the Pantheon in Greece, which were made up of individual blocks. Then, the solid bronze doors, twenty-one feet tall that weighed tons, with their interesting bulleted detail. The coffered domed ceiling, perfectly round, was dazzling to behold. The interior had many other details, like the pillars inside, the chapel and artist Raphael's tomb. Then, of course, the hole in the ceiling, the Oculus, mysterious on how it lined up with the sky and the stars. This ancient marvel, beckoned me to visit a second time,

St. Peter's Basilica, Interior Dome

after the tour, to thoroughly digest its significance and beauty.

On that first tour, we were then led down the end of the long hallway of The Vatican Museum, and guided down the steps to The Sistine Chapel. Once your eyes adjusted from the semi-dark room, all the colors of the restoration came alive. No cameras were allowed to be snapping away due to the restoration copyright. The room was packed but you could move around freely. We had twenty minutes to thoroughly gaze at the ceiling of Michelangelo's masterpiece of the Sistine Chapel frescoes and the wall with "The Last Judgement." The colors were unbelievable and the detail was magnificent. The atmosphere was one of reverence. I had made it to see one of the greatest wonders of the world.

I felt fortunate to have traveled at that time, with all the people clustered together, because who knows when that will be allowed again due to the pandemic, that has restricted the world. I saw The Sistine Chapel in all its glory. At one point, I sat and pondered this amazing room, but also awestruck of all the people being blown away just like me.

After moving through St. Peter's Basilica, we boarded a coach and arrived at the Colosseum. We all had headsets on, and as we went through security, we had to take them out of our ears and check them in baskets, as we went through the metal detectors. As I came out the other side, my tour had quickly moved on without me. I had to convince the check point guard that I was with the the tour to let me through. Then, I heard the faint voice of Falco, our tour guide, and climbed up the huge steps to inside the lower interior of the Colosseum, where I found them again, as Falco finished a short presentation of something. Then he said, "Ok Folks. You have twenty minutes, and then we must meet on the other side. You can go to the upper level, but you can only come down on the other side."

I followed directions, went up and got my "Upper Deck Interior Photograph." I came down the other side and came out into the area immediately outside the gate, still by the building. Having the headset on, outside the gate by the building, looking for the group, I then saw no one. I heard Falco making a role call, rattling off names. Then, he came to say, "Marco, Marco? Oh Marco. Anyone seen Marco?" Now, I was doubting I was in the right place. I was suddenly in a panic. If I missed getting reconnected with the group, I would miss the whole second tour. I went up the steps that led to the sidewalk by the street, hoping to see from a better distance, then ran down one end, where Falco's voice faded. Then, ran down the other side. I prayed, "God, don't let me lose this tour. Help me get back in touch with the group. Please." Finally, I heard two guys from my tour down below by the Colosseum entrance yelling and waving, "Marco! Marco!"

"Oh Thank God," I thought. They found me. My tour guide had never said, "Meet me on the inside, or meet on the outside." I was a bit embarrassed, but shook it off. I was the only one on that tour alone. Again, when by yourself on tour, you have to be on your toes, which I was, but stuff can still happen. I was relieved to be back with the group.

After the Colosseum at the end of the first tour, Falco, our tour guide in Rome, led us on the second excursion of the day, The Highlights of Rome Walking Tour, that took us through the neighborhoods that connected three marvelous sites. Starting with The Piazza Navona, where upon arriving the oval courtyard, that used to be the location for the chariot races, like in "Ben-Hur," it displayed Bernini's incredible statues and

The Colosseum Interior, Upper Deck

clustered in three main areas. One on each end and in the center. We had twenty minutes to grab a sandwich or gelatos, but I had only that much time, among all the crowds, to get my photographs as well. I raced and rushed to get my captured images. I was definitely working harder than anyone else. It was not the best scenario or the best time of day for lighting with the overhead sun, but I managed to get a few decent shots. I thought I might return to Navona on my last day. It would all depend on how much time was left. I would have to leave time at the end of my last day to get the rooftop statues at St. Peter's if I was lucky.

Next was The Pantheon. It stood out as the one place that captivated me more than any other in Rome. As we walked in through the large bronze doors, I stopped for only a few seconds and nailed one of my best photographs for my whole time in Rome. You have to be ready for the unexpected. My photojournalistic instinct took over and I framed what immediately hit me. A vertical shot, showing part of the right door, the dome and oculus centered above the chapel directly below. As we entered, Falco was talking and pointing to the ceiling, but the reception was suddenly poor on the headset, so I moved around and started snapping away.

"I could work with this. Now we're talking. Gosh! This is the place. I'm here!" I was talking to myself, and so excited. I couldn't wait to get there. I had finally made it to one of the most important places for me to see in all the world. The perfectly round coffered domed ceiling with the twenty-nine foot oculus at the top. It was mesmerizing unlike any building I had ever seen.

Not long after, I had my shots, many with the beam of light shooting in, casting a bright spot on the wall for that time of

Neptune at Piazza Navona

Pantheon Interior at Doorway

day, where it would shift with each passing hour. The tour was moving again, back out of the twenty-one foot solid bronze doors. Something inside me was saying, "You have to come back." I had tomorrow. Revisiting would be at the top of my list.

We moved back out into the Piazza Rotunda, surrounding the Pantheon and it was packed with people. The crowd was thick. We continued our walking tour, in through another neighborhood and various narrow streets, and then, suddenly, there we were at the magnificent Trevi Fountain.

We stayed on the left side because this was the most crowded site so far, and any further move closer to the center would be too much congestion to take a tour group. I also didn't want to get separated from the group like had happened back at the Colosseum, so I moved to the edge on the left three quarter side. It was a good view but I would miss capturing more of the fountain's water from a front view. It would have to wait for another time for a better shot, but for now, it was remarkable that I was even here. I was facing the sea god Oceanus directly under the arch and he was facing me.

The sculptured figures were phenomenal. I zoomed in and out, taking a variety of photos that would best capture the scene in front of me. The light was flat, and I would have to edit later, to enhance my scenes. I've seen many Trevi Fountain photos just like what I had shot, that had the main figure, Oceanus riding the waves in his chariot, facing my direction. The next time in Rome, this will be a top goal, to get the sweeping view, either at night, early morning, showing the water flowing in front, possibly holding my camera above my head in wide angle view.

After fifteen minutes, Falco, our tour guide, motioned all of us to begin walking with him, away from the Trevi, through the

The Trevi Fountain, Rome, Day II

nearby neighborhood. The two back-to-back tours had come to an end. We boarded the bus after a few blocks, and were dropped back off at the hotel. I tipped Falco a five Euro and shook his hand, and remarked, "Thank you for the great history lessons and the fantastic tour!

"Thank you," he replied.

The next morning, I took a cab back to The Pantheon at the Piazza della Rotunda, in an attempt to get exterior shots with no people. It would be quieter in the morning. The crowds accumulate midday. The cab ride was right out of a James Bond movie, with the driver racing down narrow streets, missing people and vehicles by mere inches. It was thrilling!

When I arrived around 9:00 a.m., there were hardly any people around. I got my expresso nearby, with morning bathroom break, and then went to work for the exterior shots of the Pantheon front. I succeeded in getting one of my top photos by bringing my camera down to a low angle, enough so that in the foreground, the fountain rim eliminated the view of the only man standing out in front. I made the photo near the Obelisk of Fontana del Pantheon, with a stream of water pouring from the left into the pool, while the morning sun was highlighting the Pantheon front, light slicing across its pillars, its roof and its total magnificence. At the top of the porch facade it read: "M. AGRIPPA L.F. COS TERTIUM FECIT." (Marcus Agrippa, son of Lucius, three time consul, made this).

Another photo I made left of the fountain out front, was that of a horse and carriage and one man leaning against a car, and the Pantheon building behind.

A little while later…

The Pantheon Exterior with Fountain

Forming out front for first admissions around 9:30 a.m., people started to gather. As I was standing in line, a young man asked an older man about the hole in the roof. What we got next was a local's love of The Pantheon and a history lesson. I started filming to capture the moment. In essence, what the man was saying was, "Why has this stood untouched for centuries with all the wars and all the destruction? In all of Rome, no other building can make that claim. Why?" He was asking us. Then, he pointed to the sky. "God is why. God chose to protect this building over all others. It has been preserved for a reason," the man said.

I had planned on attending mass there at 10:30 a.m., so I was killing two birds with one stone. I knew I had made the correct choice to return after hearing the man's history lesson.

The line in front of the Pantheon moved. We went in. Again, the site of the interior with the perfect dome took my breath away. I photographed it again, taking my time. I loved that I had extra time on a second visit to fully absorb this special place. The church mass would be starting in forty-five minutes. After I got my photos, I sat and got ready for the service. It was amazing I was even there, two days in a row, but now for mass? I would never forget it. It ended up being the most spectacular mass I ever experienced, with extraordinary singing and the priest giving his spirited homily in Italian. I got a few more photos after mass. Knowing I had exhausted all angles of capture with my camera, it was time for me to go.

I saw a cabbie sitting by a cab station on the right side of The Pantheon, so I leaned in and asked, "Hi, can you take me to NH Giustiniano Hotel?"

"Sure! Get in," he replied.

Then, it was another crazy James Bond ride back to the hotel.

Rooftop Angels

I couldn't afford the time to visit any new sites on the last part of my last day in Rome. When I got back to the hotel from The Pantheon, I needed lunch, so I would visit my favorite cafe for the last time. Another espresso was in store, then cut pizza with scissors and a slice of chocolate cake. What the heck! I was on vacation, so I could mix whatever I wanted for lunch.

There was one more important photograph I had to get, and I was close enough and familiar enough with the area, to aim for it. My photographer friend Ted back in the states reminded me that the sun would be setting behind the statues on the rooftop at St. Peters. So, around 3:30 p.m. I started my way over to St. Peter's Square. Somewhere I read where going up to the roof stopped around 4:30 p.m., so I had to get moving to make it in time.

It took three times to get the right information for the right area, to get in line for the roof. The line was long but it was moving. The sun would be at a good angle by the time I reached the roof, probably around 4:15 p.m.

As I had been moving about from various point A's to point B's, something indiscernible began to rise up inside of me. An intuition for something, began to get my attention. But, I had so much on my plate, that I couldn't give it a whole lot of weight. Many feelings about being here in Italy were going through me,

The Rooftop Apostles at St. Peter's Square

along with what I was seeing. It was all mashed together. It would take a few days before it would start to separate, for me to understand what the new intuition was all about.

It was now time for that last important photo to be made. It was the Rooftop Angels, but more specifically, it was Christ and his Apostles at St. Peter's Basilica rooftop edge. I was hoping to get as close as possible to them. I imagined the figures in the foreground close to me, with St. Peter's Square behind and below. Inside, I had passed by the round interior walkway just below the dome, and its remarkable mosaic walls, above St. Peter's altar below, and it led me out again to the roofline, where the Apostles and Christ statues were. I chose not to walk to the steeple from the roof, that would have been too many steps, that would have put me at the top.

When I got to the statues, they were behind a fence, and I would have to get creative with zooming and cropping to bring the statues close into my viewfinder, poking my lens through the fence bars. It would be the only way I could bring them in. The light from the late afternoon sun was sharp, giving much definition to the Apostle figures, with their backs to me, their figures against a perfect sky. They were an impressive nineteen feet tall. Working the scene, I captured the best version of what I was looking for, isolating the figures against the clouds, that included Christ the Redeemer, and the apostles to his left, St. Andrew, St. John the Evangelist and St. James the Less.

I checked all that I had shot and was happy with those last few. One of them would be the shot, from my forty-five minutes up on the roof at St. Peter's in Vatican City. I walked home to my hotel, knowing I had captured my last great photograph in Rome.

The First Italian Train

The next morning, Anna, my tour host, accompanied me as we were driven to the train station, The Roma Termini. The High Speed Rail, part of my tour package, would be taking me to Venice, the dream highpoint of my trip. We got to the gate on the upper level, as she was familiar on navigating the terminal. We sat near a cafe, and there was no time for food or drink, as we had to wait only a short while, for the schedule to post on the screens overhead, on what track my train would be departing from. Then, I would have to board quickly.

We spoke briefly on a few topics.

"How long have you been in the tourist trade?" I asked.

"About twelve years," She replied.

"How is it working for Travelgrams?" I asked, trying to make small talk. "Does it pay well?"

"It's fine. They're all about the same, more or less," she replied.

"Do you have to have a degree?"

"Usually, some have a history or teaching degree, but that's not always necessary. Experience goes a long way."

I was getting antsy and hoping it wouldn't be long.

"The track information hasn't appeared yet. It should be anytime," she said as we watched the monitors across from our stools at the terminal cafe.

Finally it appeared. I would be departing in about twenty minutes from track 4.

"Ok, you better get going," she said.

I handed Anna a twenty Euro. "Thank you so much for all your help and assistance," I told her. "It's been great to know you. An amazing time. Take care. Ciao!"

"Ciao!" She said, as I walked away.

I rolled my two pieces of luggage, one large and one small, to the train car number #7 printed on the ticket, picked up my luggage, stepped up and got inside and found my seat. It was immediately up on my right. I laughed to myself when I saw my solitary seat by the window, the last row that had the only single seat instead of two seats. It was right by the restroom. If I had to go, I wouldn't be far.

After getting settled, I clicked off a few shots before the car filled up. The train's interior looked ultra modern, like a space ship out of of "2001: A Space Odyssey," with a curvature of the seats. I was in first class, and soon, on my way to Venice. The moment before the launch was filled with excitable anticipation.

Venice. The place he dreamed of more than any other. More than Rome. There was something magically, lyrical about landing there. All the books he had studied prepared him, but also increased his desire. The more he learned, the more he wanted to know. He kept coming back to Venice. It spoke to him on a deeper level. Venice was the dream. "I have to get there someday and someday soon somehow!" he told himself. "If I went nowhere else for the rest of my life, that would be it." Venice was the place.

Twenty minutes after boarding, we shoved off. Without any jerking motion, the train just started to roll. I noticed how quiet and smooth it was, almost as if we were riding on rubber wheels.

"Wow!" he thought to himself. "This is unreal. I'm on my way to Venice, on a train through Italy. I'm really doing it! Like I always dreamed. No words describe what this is for me."

It was like a movie scene. I was just as excited to be riding the train in Italy as in seeing St. Peter's in Rome. As I rolled away, passing the Roma Termini station outside the window, I said, "Goodbye Rome. Hope to see you again someday."

He then remembered throwing three coins in the Trevi Fountain, from his right hand over his left shoulder. The first coin assured his return to Rome.

As the train moved toward Venice, my intuition was telling me that this trip was about much more than what was on the surface, more than what I thought the trip was about for me. Which was to touch and taste that place shaped like a boot, across the Atlantic for this boy so romantic, and to capture images to bring back home. But, it was so much more, to the degree I had no idea. It was enough just to keep up with my day to day, hour by hour goals I had set for myself, and the three half day tours that gave me an introductory history. However, something else was evolving, ever so slowly. If it would have been given to me all at once, it would have blown my mind.

The cart appeared on my left, as I was the first seat from my end of the car, and in Italian accent, the train attendant asked if I wanted coffee or something to drink. "Caffe? Something to drink?" he asked.

"Si, Yes. Coffee," I replied.

The train attendant was well dressed in tailored train uniform. He poured quick and accurately in a printed cup and gave me a cookie, also in its perfectly packaged wrapper with great photograph and graphics. Then he rolled the food and beverage cart to the next few rows after I said "Grazie."

I was like a little kid at my first carnival, filled with excitement, wondering, "What's next?" It was early and I needed the coffee. When I took that first sip, I couldn't get over how good it was, from a food and beverage cart on an Italian train. The cookie was just as good or was it because I was in Italy. "No, they were better than average at most things. "Art, Architecture, Music, Food. All better than average when in Italy. Coffee and cookie from a train.

We stopped at a variety of towns on the way to Venice. It would be a four hour ride. Half the day. Watching through the window at the train stops, I observed everything; the look of the platform, the location surrounding it, the people waiting, the Italian graffiti. Where were they all going? I couldn't imagine what it would be like living there, having access to this whole amazing country, probably the most beautifully ornate country in all the world. At least that is what I have come to understand from all the photographs I had ever seen, and now, from what I'm in the middle of, confirms to me, the unrivaled, unspeakable beauty, that tagged on my heart, telling me for years now...

"Come see me. Come touch me. You need me, and I need you, because we have a journey to take together. There's much for you to see and learn." Italy told Marco that, long before he came. The words just hadn't formed yet, but it had been a long aching in his heart.

Now, he was there in the middle of it. It was unfolding unlike anything else in his life. He had just gotten started, and captured so much already. It would be six months before he would fully realize how great the images were, that he had captured in his three days in Rome. He worried that they might have missed their mark, in the caliber of excellence he sought to achieve, with his camera.

He nailed five images in black and white, that would serve as the greatest reminder, displayed on his living room wall, the dream of Rome, come to life. They were: "Castel Sant'Angelo" and Bernini's Bridge of Angels; "Interior of The Colosseum," a wide shot from the upper deck; The Pantheon, Interior at Doorway, captured in split-second timing, as he walked in while on tour; "The Pantheon Exterior with Fountain," with no people, captured the following morning, with sunlight striped across the columns in front, and lastly, "The Rooftop Apostles at St. Peter's Square," at the Vatican, his last photograph made before leaving Rome.

On his way to Venice, Marco would just need to remember to keep one foot in front of the other, his shot list to guide him, his prayers to keep him safe and also give him last minute reminders of what to capture, what would be the best places to focus on. Even though he had a whole extra day in Venice, four days in all, he had to use every moment wisely, to make the best of his opportunity.

The train rolled on, clickety-clack, a slight swaying left to right, but he was moving forward. He would send up a prayer, to the One who got him there,

"Thank you Lord, for this most incredible time of my life. I don't know what to say, or how to thank you enough. But, thank you so much for getting me here. These images I dream of getting…Please let me get them next in Venice. I've waited so long, for this trip to come," Marco lifted up his prayer to Jesus, his friend through thick and thin, since 1977, when something miraculous happened, putting him on a new path, right before photography school, many years ago. There were many hard roads in between, over the years. With all that early difficulty behind him, and years of healing, he was at his best now, more than ever, to make the most of it.

The views out his train window told so many stories. This was heartland Italy he was riding through. There were the interesting agricultural patterns of farmland he had never seen in the states. Buildings close to the tracks that the train would pass, that had interesting designs. Before he could study it, they were gone, the train moving too fast. Different in their roofs, the external sides, the windows. Even the most humble of structures were built differently in Italy. That's what made the train ride so interesting. He also saw older train cars parked and abandoned, with Italian graffiti on their sides and on the train station walls.

He would see roads stretched out from the uncluttered overpasses to the small towns and wonder, "What's life like there? What's life like anywhere in Italy?"

"I'm on my way to Venice. Man! I can't believe where I'm going and how much I just experienced in Rome. What a whirlwind! I'll be there in a few hours. What I'm in the middle of, is something hard to believe. It's my life's greatest dream," Marco's thought as the bullet train rocketed on at 125 mph across the Italian landscape.

Wherever he was going, he always reviewed the shot list, and how best to capture the areas and the subject. Different subjects required different approaches and treatments. All his years of experience, decades as a photographer and artist, were being called upon with his toolkit of techniques and tips. Lens

On the Way to Venice

type, distance to subject, f-stop, horizontal or vertical, what to emphasize, what to minimize, color vs. black and white. He learned to zero in on what first attracted him to a scene, then unclutter it. His was a clean, vintage style. The subject had to always stand out, separated and brought into prominence from uncluttered backgrounds, whenever possible.

He went in search of more than he really understood. The trip would change his life. He didn't know it yet, but something was coming, the deeper reason on why it was important for him to cross the Atlantic, to go so far, to the country he felt the greatest love for, beyond all the photographs he would work hard to make. Those images didn't just happen. He had to use all his skill, talent and readiness, to make an image worthy of his collection. He would have to examine and study each scene and opportunity, to go through his process to land the best version of what was in front of him and his lens.

Sometimes, it was lackluster, not what he had hoped for. Other times, he reviewed over and over the images and realized what he had captured were strikingly special, or could grow on him over time. Some images were surprises and instantly recognized as a "Best" that would be forever etched, from his first trip to Italy, like "The Pantheon Interior at Doorway" he captured as he was walking in with the tour, into the most magnificent structure in Rome. Now, it takes its place as a new treasure, from his very first view of the Pantheon interior. Was it luck? No, he was ready. Preparation met opportunity with all the years of shooting fleeting action, of performers in constant motion at rock concert stages, using manual focus. Then, years as a corporate photographer, capturing news making events, not knowing how the events would unfold upon arrival, so he was always on his toes, ready.

Other photographs that made the grade, he had more time to compose, like the interior from the upper deck of Rome's Colosseum, that he specifically composed in black an white.

All the train stops along the way to Venice, allowed him to study the platforms and the people. The bored ones were the locals. The ones that scurried were visitors from afar, like Marco, wondering, "Ok, What's next? How can I best be ready for the next thing, to cross my path? What should I review before I get to the next stop?

He was getting close. The train had just passed through Padua and then Bologna. Soon, he felt the train curve and he saw the large body of water and then he saw IT, Venice, with the long bridge connecting him to his long awaited dream.

"This is it. Man. Gosh. This has to be the greatest wonder of my life. Venice."

Landing in Venice

He was getting choked up a bit, his eyes getting teary. It meant so much.

The train was slowing down, then he heard the conductor's announcement, "Buongiorno Venezia Santa Lucia."

People started rising from their seats, immediately reaching for their bags and luggage.

I checked my large photo bag near my feet and brought it up close to me, checking with a glance that all was in place, taking the ear buds out, returning them with the iPod to their quaint little case. Everything in its place. It had paid to research all the messenger style photo bags I bought for my trip, and they ended up being perfect, not giving away how much golden gear I was carrying, but a bag strong, smart and fully organized.

The conductor made another announcement, "Buongiorno Santa Lucia!" The train came to a final halt. People were now in line ready to exit.

My thoughts, as I grabbed my two suitcases, "I'm here. I'm in Venice. Gosh. This is surreal."

"Stay sharp Marco," he told himself, as he fastened the strap around his waist that would prevent anyone from trying to grab his camera bag off his shoulder.

I got in the line that was moving to exit the train. Stepping down, I rolled my luggage to where the end of the track platform met the main thoroughfare. Next, I was to meet my Travelgram Tour Host Franco.

I rolled my luggage up and down the main drag at the Santa Lucia Train Station and saw no one holding a sign, looking for me. I needed the restroom and found one not far around the corner. It was one Euro dollar to enter, with clear gates that would swing up when you entered the coin in the slot. "Strange," I thought. But, it made sense in a place like this. At least the conditions were clean. I rolled my two bags in tandem after I was allowed entry after my coin. Exiting the bathroom, I looked for Franco again over on the main hallway.

"Not sure if this guy is going to show. I'll give it a little more time. If I have to walk to the hotel myself, at least they said it was only a three minutes away," I thought.

I walked up and down again a few more times, then I saw a guy holding a sign. I walked over and approached him, seeing the "Travelgrams" on the sign and I said, "Travelgrams? Franco? Hotel Abbazia?"

"Yes, Your name?" He asked.

"Marco Conte," I replied.

"Ok. We have one more. We'll wait a few more minutes. If he doesn't show before long, we'll walk over. The hotel is very close-a."

"Ok. Thank you," I said.

Three minutes later…
No one was showing.

"Ok, we'll go. I can come back to check in a few minutes."

We walked out of the train station and down the steps and I got my first sight of Venice. It was like a picture postcard. The

Grand Canal was right out in front of the train station. Boats were driving by and ornate street lamps framed the scene. I would return to duplicate this first view I was seeing from the top of the steps of the Santa Lucia Train Station.

"This is unreal. I'm in Venice!" I thought to myself.

It was crowded, as we made an immediate left from The Santa Lucia Train Station steps, past vendors and the vaparetto stop along The Grand Canal on the right, and The Scalzi Church on the left. Then, we walked past The Scalzi Bridge on the right, one of only four bridges in all of Venice to span The Grand Canal, to the main islands. As we pushed through the crowd, straight ahead were shops and restaurants, and it was lunchtime and packed with people, locals and tourists. I followed Franco, my tour host, as he rolled my smaller luggage bag in front of me. We made a quick left onto a narrow alley street, Calle Priuli Del Caveletti, and in only a minute's walk, we came to Hotel Abbazia on the left, a centuries old monastery, that once housed a regularly visiting Pope Pius X, confirmed with a commemorative plaque in the lobby.

Now, he had arrived into the heart of it, the deeper part of his Italy that he had dreamed about. What he was really moving into now, was the second phase of his journey. Unbeknownst to Marco, there would be three phases in all. He was getting closer to something, an underbelly. An unfolding that had been part of his life.

There was a whole new itinerary. It would take a few hours, maybe a day, for him to get his bearings. Marco now felt more in tune here. Rome had been amazing in a different, historical way, with just scratching the surface there. But, it was in Venice that he was most in awe of, and with an extra day there, he would work hard to make it count, to see and experience the ornate

First View of Venice from Santa Lucia Train Station

beauty of the places like, Piazza San Marco and everything around it, but more than anything, to make life changing everlasting images to bring back home.

Later, he would recover a part of himself lost years ago, that he had forgotten about. His heart and soul part of Italy, that would return, from this amazing trip, that he was bold enough to take alone.

After I was checked into the hotel, which had no elevator, I found my room, after huffing it up the stairs with my luggage, and settled in for a few minutes, taking a few moments to think about what was next.

Examining the room, with its rustic wooden beams on the ceiling, and windows that opened into a quiet courtyard not easily seen. My photographer friend Ted from the states, had just sent me a message that told me of a single train route leaving Venice to Pescara, that I would take next, so I wouldn't need to change trains in Bologna. With my current two train route that was originally set up from the travel lady Caroline, it would have been too short a transfer from Venice. I became uncomfortable with the idea of changing trains to get to my grandfather's hometown region.

"You should go to the train station ticket office and see if you can get it changed," Ted had said.

Recognizing this new information for the train change, I went right back to the Venezia Santa Lucia Train Station first thing, and got in line for ticketing.

The ticket clerk was able to change that two train route from Venice to Bologna, Bologna to Pescara into one train, Venice to Pescara, but he was not able to change the two train route from Pescara back to Rome. It would be Pescara to further South Foggia, then Foggia back up to Rome Termini, then Rome

Termini to Rome Airport on that last day. It would be all day on the trains, because Pescara was not a main travel hub in Italy. The main issue was getting the one train from Venice to Pescara.

"Ok," I said. "I'll take the single train to Pescara. Are you able to keep me in first class?"

"No, sorry, that will be a second class train, but I'll put you in the middle of the car, close to the luggage. It will be fine," the train clerk said.

"Ok, Grazie!" I said.

I paid the up charge difference for the train change. Now, I wouldn't have to worry about missing the train connection on the way to my grandfather's hometown region.

"Ahhh, I'm so glad I got that worked out. Now, I can get on with my day and venture out and see what's immediately in my neighborhood.

I lingered in the Hotel Abbazia for about twenty minutes, as it was interesting in its quietness and decor in the lobby, which had been a monastery meeting place with a pulpit, and a commemorative plaque of Pope Pius X.

I snapped a few pics in the immediate area outside the hotel, the narrow street it was on, Calle Priuli Del Caveletti, then ventured out into the main street, stepping first into the Scalzi Church, which is called St. Mary of Nazareth. It was impressive, a masterpiece of Venetian Baroque period, with its Carrara, white marble facade, realized between 1672 and 1680, and inside, detailed medium chapels flanked right and left of main chapel, and four smaller chapels divided on right and left.

I took a half-dozen photographs of the church interior, then ventured back outside.

I was attracted to the Scalzi Bridge that had stone pillared railings, wide steps and so, I was curious for my first view from the top, overlooking The Grand Canal. I walked to its peak, and took in the view, while motorboats passed underneath me. The view was so striking, and in every direction, a postcard view, that I could barely absorb it all. The only way I knew to begin my navigation in Venice was through my camera. I would let it guide me.

Not ready to venture too far off, or even to the other side of the bridge, I came back down and made an immediate right toward where all the action was, straight ahead on the main drag in Cannaregio, Rio Terra Lista Di Spagna. There were shops galore along with restaurants and pizza parlors. I had to be thinking of when to eat, as tomorrow morning was the half-day tour of the Doge Palace, St. Mark's Basilica and Murano Glass Factory. I would be introduced to the area surrounding St. Mark's Square. For now, I was venturing out to get familiar with the immediate neighborhood, and navigating in Venice by myself, brought its own challenges.

Just to be here in Venice on my own, was such an accomplishment in itself. I had faith that I would accomplish more photos here, now that I had success behind me from the photos I had taken in Rome.

But, as exciting going into Venice was, it was overwhelming. Where would I begin? All those canals and bridges? The vaporetto water buses. I didn't know how those worked yet. It wouldn't take long before I knew how to navigate. You don't just jump off a train from one city to another, in a strange country, and start snapping away. One has to get acclimated to the new area, to get a "feel" for the place.

I thought it best on my remaining first day, to stay close to hotel in the neighborhood. My instincts helped me with that too, when not to venture far. Some areas would speak louder than others. I would know when and what would be worthy of photographs. As always, I lifted up my prayers to ask for blessings on getting great photos, but also for safety, and anything else I needed to be aware of.

"Thank you Lord, for getting me here. Guide me, protect me and let me get these photos I dream of. Thank you," Marco lifted up.

The day was getting late and I saw a restaurant that looked decent to settle on for dinner. It was Poveledo. I got cleaned up and arrived during a busy dinner hour.

I had noticed my cellphone began acting buggy back in Rome, with the power draining quickly, even though I had bought a cellphone charging block, but something else was going wrong.

"One Sir?" A waiter asked, approaching me while I waited to be seated.

"Yes," I replied.

He walked me through the whole length of the empty restaurant, until we reached the outside patio that was nearly full with people. When he walked me to my table, it was right on The Grand Canal with an incredible view.

"Looks like I picked a winner," I thought. "This is amazing."

I felt happy and sad, as I sat down in the most picturesque dinner setting ever. I took a few snaps with my cellphone camera as the soft glow of late afternoon sun was fading just before the beginning of twilight, with orange lanterns strung along the edge of the patio, and a gondolier was gliding by on this magnificent canal. I made the photograph as he passed by. A most perfect scene.

I was sad, only momentarily, because I was alone, and all around me were couples enjoying each others' company in this

First Dinner in Venice, on the Grand Canal

romantic setting. Yet, I was happy, because I was here in Italy, in Venice, and now at this restaurant, despite the temporary awkwardness of being alone, I felt good that I had the courage to take this trip by myself, and I was filled with a peace, because something else was telling me, that there was some greater purpose for my being here. I'm sure I wasn't the only one who ever traveled to Italy alone, or even dined alone on The Grand Canal in Venice.

It took courage. Part of that happiness told me, this was something not everyone could do alone. But, I did, and phase one was behind me with amazing photos I had made in Rome.

The dinner was a great one. Shrimp Scampi in red sauce and a small Pizza Margherita. I left full, from a great meal and grand experience.

Now, it was nightfall. As I ventured down the main drag, I came to wider clearing with more vendors, but a church adjacent to another large building caught my eye, with its architectural elements and spot lighting. With my Sony a6300 and its ultra sensitive night vision, I clicked off a few photos in black and white. Up ahead, I saw the edge of the water by another canal, and was attracted to a possible better nighttime scene with stationary gondolas parked on my side and buildings across the spotlit water.

I found and settled on a scene of two guys across the other side underneath a bar street lamp. They left quickly, but it left the scene with a gondola in front of me, the water and buildings beyond it, and I captured my last scene of my first evening in Venice.

As I got back to the hotel, to get ready for the morning tour, I realized something screwy was going on with my phone. The

Nighttime Gondola, First Evening in Venice

power drain had begun in Rome. Now, a small pop up screen suddenly appeared on top of all my apps, preventing me from using all my programs, and this glitch was not going away, with no way to shut down the phone and reboot.

"What the hell. Great. The phone stops working right before my tour in the morning," I said to myself out loud.

Keyed up from this, it was approaching midnight, and my phone, which had been my main alarm clock, was no longer reliable.

I quickly ran down to the front desk of the hotel to arrange a wake up call. The hotel clerk couldn't speak English. But, he understood enough when I said, "Per Favore, 6:30 a.m. Wake Up Call. Room 410?"

"Si! 6:30. Room 410," he said as he understood.

"Si, 6:30. Room 410," I repeated. "Grazie." I would have to trust that I would be wakened at the correct time.

Back in my room, I messed around with the phone and I was able to click the pop up screen away for a few seconds at a time in order to set my alarm. I had a new problem going into tomorrow, an important day of the tour of the Doge Palace, St. Mark's Basilica and Murano Glass Factory. I would need a brand new cellphone. Something I wasn't counting on.

Halfway around the world, for a particular amount of time, about twenty hours, family and friends would have no idea if I was living or dead. I had been communicating all along with my brothers, a buddy in Cleveland, a friend in Charlotte, and some people on Facebook and Messenger. With no working phone to communicate using texting, email, Wi-Fi and internet connection, I was cut off, like back in the 90's. Now, I was feeling even more alone, in a country where I was the foreigner, outside my native land and language.

"Get the Horses, Then the Phone"

Venice was the center point, where a shift had begun.
A shift of amazing serendipities.

At 6:30, the wake up call came in, and a few minutes later, my unusable cellphone also rang. It would be the last thing it would give me in Italy. Now it was dead. But, I was grateful for the wake-up call and the tour was on, and my day was alive. My camera and I would be ready to seek images during this rare opportunity on this once-in-a-lifetime tour in Venice: that of The Doge Palace, St. Mark's Basilica, The Bridge of Sighs and Murano Glass Factory.

Those of us on the tour, all met in the hotel lobby at 8:30 a.m. and Franco, our tour host, ushered us to a motorboat that would take us down The Grand Canal.

I stood up in the motorboat, so I could see everything out in front, as we shoved off. I remember watching everything I could take in along the way down to St. Mark's Square. The activity along the canal in the Venetian morning was in full swing, like deliveries by boats to various docks. We were seeing everyday life unfold in this city on the water, this city of dreams.

It was a murky, overcast day for starters, but later the sun would pierce through the clouds for directional light. We arrived after a fifteen minute boat ride. After it docked, we were led through a string of narrow streets, past the Bacino Orseolo, the gondola station, where I snapped a cluster of gondolas all snug together. Then, we came out and suddenly we were in Piazza San Marco.

"Wow! I'm really here!" I thought to myself. I was now at the place I had studied so many times, from all the photos, from all my books. I was struck by this famous place, and immediately I was thinking how I would choose to photograph it. There it stood in the distance, with its unique architecture, that was a combination of Western European and Byzantine ideas, with its onion domes, turrets and mosaics, flanked by the church bell tower, the Campanile, on the right. We walked closer and past it, and I was overwhelmed at the sight and a thousand ideas raced through my head.

We walked to the corner, near St. Mark's Basin, and met Rosetta, our tour guide, in front of The Doge Palace, the most extensive part of our tour.

She was an interesting character, full of poise and a classy smile. What I noticed most was her end of sentence intonation, where every word ended with an "ah". When I asked her about it, further into our tour, she remarked, "Yes, Venetian dialect is unique blend of Spanish, Italian and Venetian.

Franco, our tour host who had brought us, and left us with Rosetta, also had that same intonation, that I began to notice, after I zeroed in on the dialect with Rosetta.

"I will see you all later at Murano Glass Factory-a, at end of tour-a," he said.

We got our headsets on and we entered the Doge Palace entrance, then up the outside steps to the second level, with fantastic views through multiple portico arches and pillars, looking down onto the courtyard. We paused outside a doorway where Rosetta explained about the "mouth of truth," a face in the wall that swallow complaints or suspicions, on pieces of paper. We then entered up the steps of the Golden Staircase with the 24-carot gold ceiling into the first series of rooms.

The paintings on the frescoed walls and ceilings by artists like Tintoretto were phenomenal. It was an excessive showcase of The Doge's power of the Republic in all of Europe. We came to the largest room, the Grand Council Chamber, that was enormous in scale, and is the largest room in the world that has no support columns. On the far end of the room, displayed the world's largest oil painting, Tintoretto's "Paradise," and a total of twenty-one paintings in that room alone, were displayed by the artist.

We made our way across The Bridge of Sighs, and past the prison cells, where the guilty and convicted would catch their last sight of the outside world, through the mosaic windows, uttering their last sighs.

As we were getting ready to leave, I used the restroom. The window was open and I caught a glimpse of the Bridge of Sighs right close by outside the window. I leaned out and snapped two photos.

As we walked outside to the courtyard from the doorway of The Doge Palace, I made another photo of a great scene above the doorway we had exited, that of The Winged Lion (St. Mark) and The Doge holding a flag facing each other. It was surreal in its scale of the two figures in relationship to each other, with the winged lion overwhelming in size to the doge.

I wouldn't notice this scene in detail until I was back home in Ohio. Luckily, even though it was the only photo I got of that ornate doorway and two figures, it was sharp enough that I could extract the best essence of that detailed doorway with The Doge and Winged Lion, in a cropped photo, that would

View of St. Mark's from Doge Palace

eventually hang on my wall.

We walked through the courtyard, past the outside "Stairway of Giants," where centuries before, people came to approach The Doge at the top of the stairs, who would be standing between the statues of Mars, The God of War and Neptune, The God of Sea. They had been built in the fifteenth century.

Every so often that day, I thought of my uncertainty of what kind of struggle it would be to get a new cellphone after this tour was over. Where would there even be a cellphone shop? For now, I would push that aside and trust it would all work out later on, for me to have a working phone again. There might be people worried about me after some time. For now, I needed to take it all in, on the tour and get as many photos as possible. Where others on our tour group were just watching, observing and listening, I was busy working, anticipating every possible photographic possibility on every part of the tour presented and shown, living the experience through my lenses. It would help engrave my experiences on a deeper level than passive observation.

We came to reassemble with tour host Rosetta, in the front of St. Mark's Basilica, then we got a walk through the Basilica interior that was covered in gold. It was kind of dark, as we snaked through the pre-guided route and came out the other side. I was a bit disappointed on the "no photo" policy inside, and it wasn't worth testing by stealing a photo or two.

Next, for the last part of our tour, we walked a little ways, beyond St. Mark's Square, through a few streets and over a small bridge and came to The Murano Glass Factory and Museum. We got to see an artisan glassblower make a horse in less than five minutes. I got up and took a few photos close to

The Doge Facing St. Mark, The Winged Lion

him, until I was told by a guy behind me, "You're blocking everyone's view." Sometimes you have to take risks to get photographs, even at the discomfort of others. I quickly moved out of the way, after I got my shots.

At almost the end of our tour of The Murano Glass Factory, we were led into a showroom where a sales representative gave us a quick demonstration on how strong the glass was by banging a glass bowl onto a glass slab on a table. "Whack! Whack!" As she pounded the glass sharply down, she said, "If I kept hitting this and it would break, I'd lose my job. But, you can see how much stronger this glass is. It would eventually break, but it is stronger."

I sat right in front of her. When she was done I asked, "Do you have any espresso cups?"

"We do," she said. "We have white gold inlay and yellow gold inlay espresso cups," as she pulled the white gold inlay cup down, for me to see closer, with a matching saucer.

"Wow. So exquisite," I pondered.

"How much for this?" I asked.

"$150 Euros for a single with matching saucer and $50 for shipping. But, if you buy two, the shipping is free and $290 Euros for the set."

I thought how I had never bought anything that extravagant before. That was changing right here, right now.

"Ok, I'll take the two," I said.

"Would you like them engraved?" She asked.

"How much for that?"

"No charge," she said.

"Sure," I answered.

The engraved saucers would eventually read, "Marco Conte First Trip To Venice 2019."

St. Mark's Basilica, Front View

She started to put them in a silk lined gift box when I asked, "How much?"

"Oh, I throw this in. No charge," she said with a smile.

So, for a bit over $300 US dollars, the value of what those cups would bring me was priceless. When would I ever visit again? It would always remind me how special Venice was, the city I got to see and experience in four days. Some things you can't put a price tag on. I would never forget this and the white inlay espresso cups would always remind me of the tour.

Shortly after, we were free to go, and we were on our own, with each of us having to find our own way back to the hotel, which the vaporetto would allow, only I had another main agenda after the tour in Venice. I had to find a phone shop. Franco, our tour host, had turned up at the end of our tour, just to see we all had made it through. When I asked him about a phone shop, he showed me on the map, how there was only one cellphone shop in all of Venice. I found that information suspect. "A kickback maybe?" I thought.

I walked away from St. Mark's Square, along the water's edge where a cluster of vendors were stationed. It was part amusement park with souvenirs and food. The weather was great, with the sun high in the sky, and I saw a gelato shop. It seemed the perfect time to take a break. I needed to regroup.

As I was enjoying my chocolate and pistachio gelato, continuing my flavor tradition from Rome, watching the passersby, I struck up a conversation with a guy next to me.

"How you doing?" I asked.

He tilted his head in hello fashion with a slight smile.

"Can you tell me where I might find a cellphone shop?" I asked.

"They're all over," he answered.

"Really? My tour host told me there was only one shop in all of Venice, but I thought that was suspect," I said.

"That's baloney. He's probably telling you that to give a kickback to somebody."

"Yeah, right.

Ok, thanks," I said.

Now, knowing the tour host wasn't giving me the accurate run down on cellphone shops, I felt better knowing that I would just have to start walking into the heart of the city, on the other side of St. Mark's Square, and look and ask.

First, I had to photograph the horses on top of St. Mark's Basilica balcony. I waited until about 3:00 p.m. and walked over and got in line. I had a short window to get the photos and also allow time to find a phone shop. I was still cut off from the rest of the world without it. The photographs were first in importance, a top bucket list photo, then getting reconnected to family and friends was second.

Fifteen minutes later, I was in the upper inside chamber of St. Mark's Basilica, viewing the original Triumphal Quadriga, the four Roman bronze statues of horses that were placed on the loggia above the porch, after the sack of Constantinople in 1204. They remained there until Napoleon looted them in 1797, but then they were returned to Venice in 1815. Inside, the horses were spotlit and spectacular! There was a tour guide explaining the history of these amazing bronze sculpted horses, to a small group of people. I stood and examined the detail, but couldn't linger long. I was anxious to get out on the roof to make my photographs of the four horses out on the balcony, the replicas, above St. Mark's Square.

As I walked out onto the balcony atop the church's facade, I was expecting a crowd of people, with limited time and viewpoint to get my photos. Before long, after only a handful people had come and gone, I was the only one left up there and I had free reign to take my bucket list photos of those beautiful horses. That in itself was a miracle. It could have been really crowded and that would have seriously restricted my shooting.

Then, I thought, "Gosh, I'm here." All the months of studying the photos of St. Mark's Basilica, this was the one photo I wanted more than anything in Venice.

You never know what you will encounter and there's always a challenge, so you try to solve the problem of whatever is in the way of what you want to capture with a camera, to achieve in a scene.

In the twelve years working as a corporate photographer, covering five states for corporate communications, Marco had encountered many unpredictable shooting scenarios, where he learned to solve the problems and challenges quickly, to capture the images needed, for publication deadlines.

There was a white gauze-like material covering the horses' hooves on their pedestals. This would be my challenge, as I was forced to crop it out. Losing that part of the horse, with their hooves touching the ground, I had to find a way to capture the integrity of the horses, getting the best angle, while cropping out the horses hooves on the pedestals and the white gauze material. This was initially disappointing, but I kept on zeroing in, getting more of the essence of the scene. Shooting in both directions, toward the clock tower first, then toward St. Mark's Basin after, I landed my best photo with the horses facing the Campanile, the Bell Tower on the right, with leg and hoof in the air prominently in galloping position. The wide angle lens captured an exaggerated airborne hoof. The bell tower is leaning toward the position of the horse, and the horse is

The Bronze Horses atop St. Mark's Basilica

galloping toward the tower, and those elements are perfectly compressed and in juxtaposition to each other. Shooting in black and white mode allowed me to see those tonal values without color, through my viewfinder, that aided my composition.

What began as a disappointment with gauze covered hooves, just became a problem to solve. I kept working the scene until I had exhausted all possibilities. When I felt I could shoot no more, It was time to leave. The time I spent up on the roof of St. Mark's with the four horses was well over an hour. I had worked the scene well.

I took one last shot, that of the piazza below, also in black and white, showing the whole ground expanse of "the drawing room,"as they called the large square, considered by many as having some of the greatest architecture in the world. I shot the scene below, with people in shadow, and it looked like it could have been captured in the 50's, a timeless image. Then, I was finished.

The Walk to Cannaregio

Now, I had to move fast to find a cellphone shop. I would be at the mercy of the Venetian strangers to help guide me, but I sent up a prayer too, for assurance that I would find what I needed.

"God, Please help me find a cellphone shop, and the phone I need to have."

Without my cellphone, I was transported back to how it was in the 1990's. Thirty years behind without technology in my pocket. How much we take for granted now, with our current technology. My main reason for a new phone was to let family and friends know that I was ok. I didn't want them to worry.

Walking through the heart of Venice, along a narrow street filled with passing people, I heard a young man speaking good English, when mostly everything else I heard all around me was Italian. I saw he was with his family and so I blurted out, "There's someone speaking really good English."

His father acknowledged me and nodded, "Hello."

"Excuse me," I continued. "I was wondering if you happened to see a cellphone shop anywhere? My phone died last night and I have to get another phone."

"Actually, I just saw one from where we came. I can point you in the right direction," the man said.

"That would be really great," I replied.

We walked out into a small piazza where a few narrow streets veered off.

"Right up here," he pointed to a narrow street that turned left by a bar. "If you go down a ways, it's on the left. If you don't find it, I should be at this bar for a little while."

"Hey, thank you," I said.

I prayed that the cellphone shop would be there and that it would be open. It was. The Tele Radio Shop was on Calle de la Mandola.

The man operating the shop knew enough English to get me set up with a new phone. I got there at 5:00 p.m and we spent ten minutes or so trying to understand each other. Then, I settled on the right phone, with us going over everything and getting the SIMM card and my 64 GB memory card installed, from the phone that had failed me, that had all my cellphone photos taken up to that point from Rome and first twenty hours of Venice. After an hour, and $140 Euros later, I walked out of there with an Italian cellphone and flipbook case. It gave me WI-FI, internet, email, GPS and a great camera. That Italian phone saved me and got me home that evening with GPS guiding me through the streets.

Before I started back, I was hungry and stopped at Rosso Pomodoro, a restaurant that had a pizza bar by the counter. I had a thoroughly enjoyable personal size margherita pizza and cappuccino. It was great to watch all the activity coming and going, and the other part of the restaurant behind a glass wall. It ended up being a top place I ducked into for a quick bite to eat, at the height of dinner hour.

I decided to walk all the way back to the hotel as I was getting good directions from the Android Google lady who rattled off long Italian street names in a British accent. "Turn left at Calle Cavalli past Campo Manin." I had come out to a small piazza clearing and there was the memorial for Daniele Manin, an Italian Patriot who was a key figure for reorganizing Venice, a hero of the Italian unification, I would later learn. His statue sat on a pedestal above a large winged lion. It was an impressive sight so I took a photograph. I would stop along the walk home, numerous times and capture more scenes.

As I moved on, I felt safe and calm, and I was in tune with where I was going that day in Venice, Italy. Here, I was in a foreign country, walking the streets of Venice alone, with just a phone to guide me. I would just aim my phone, listen to the British speaking Google lady announce the street names and direction, look for the street sign on the buildings, which sometimes was hard to read or find, and watch where everyone else was walking. My sense of direction instincts filled in the cracks.

I walked as far as I could to the Rialto Bridge dock, then, a small jaunt on the vaporetto got me to the other side, where I got off at San Marcuola, one stop early, where I could walk and explore more, leaving me only a mile or two left to finally make it home to Hotel Abbazia in Cannaregio. I had walked from one end of Venice to the other, by myself. It was quite an accomplishment. The whole day became epic and I would have photographs to last a lifetime.

The unexpected turn of events of losing my phone and getting a new one, forced me to improvise and push through new challenges, despite anxious moments. Getting a bit lost on the way home that day, I wouldn't have traded it for anything. The discoveries I made with my camera, made that walk home unforgettable. It was rich beyond compare.

Daniele Manin and Winged Lion

Rio Marin, on the Walk Home

Solo Gondola

On my third day in Venice, I arrived at St. Mark's Square mid-morning and arranged on the fly, a solo gondola ride. The gondoliers all negotiate whatever they feel like on a given day, but usually between $80-$100 Euros. It was pricey, but worth every penny for the experience. It was priceless, for the photos the gondola ride allowed me to make.

I met my gondolier, Angelo, at St. Mark's Basin. His rate was $100 Euros for forty minutes. We shoved off from the square at 10:25 a.m. I was able to move about in the boat to get the right viewpoints from my camera, with the tip of the gondola boat out in front of me in the foreground scene, and shots of Angelo behind me working his oar, moving the boat.

We came out of St. Mark's Square and did an arc and went under the first bridge that was in front of The Doge Palace and immediately after, we approached from below, the famous Bridge of Sighs, which I had walked through the day before on tour. The light was diffuse but directional. I took a step back and paused for a minute from my camera to soak up the moment, with the smooth ride and the quietness of the boat, moving down the narrow canals. It was beautifully surreal.

We moved toward the end of the Castello section, not quite to the Rialto Bridge, and then made a turn-a-round, returning back from where we came.

Solo Gondola Ride, in Quiet Canals

Angelo said, "Up here, up on the right, Casanova lived." Not long after, he pointed out another building. "Here, Marco Polo lived." I snapped quite a few photos and I made the best of the experience, framing the boat, in lower part of the frame, with whatever scene was in front of me.

I asked Angelo, "How long have you been a gondolier?"

"Thirty-nine years," he replied. "I learned from my father, my uncle and my grandfather."

I made sure to take a few photos with my Italian cellphone besides my Sony camera. It would record the GPS location tag that I could review later in Google Maps, on where I had gone on the gondola.

We came through the canal that took us back under the Bridge of Sighs, swinging out in an arc, in St. Mark's Basin again. I took as many photographs as I could, as we swung back around in front of St. Mark's Square, rowing back up to the dock. I got out and thanked Angelo, tipping him a few Euros in a hat that rested on the dock.

He had said it would be forty minutes, but it ended up being only thirty minutes. I didn't feel cheated. It was still worth the money spent for an unforgettable experience. Now, I had photographs that I would always treasure from that once in a lifetime experience of my solo gondola boat ride in Venice. Another bucket list photograph had been captured and checked off with great satisfaction.

Gondolier Angelo Steering at St. Mark's Bay

Beauty at Florian Caffe

After my gondola ride, I hung around St. Mark's Square, returning to the gondola boats, along the edge, looking out toward San Giorgio Maggiore and Giudecca, the quintessential Venice scene that captivated me over and over. I would return to photograph this view four times.

Walking into St. Mark's Square, I was drawn to the famous Florian Caffe, the oldest coffeehouse in all of Italy and Europe. As I write this, the caffe is now three hundred years old. The orchestra band played right outside and I knew I had to experience this ornate palace of coffee delights, with the rich history. After all, Charles Dickens and Giuseppe Verdi dined here.

I entered the Florian and was led down the hallway to the last room and seated at a table directly at the end of the hallway. It was a treat just to be seated there. Each room had a theme. Mine was the Moorish Room, that displayed antique paintings of Asian beauties. The gold, frescoed walls were the same as when they opened it in 1720. The marble tables also were from centuries before. The waiters were immaculately dressed. Classy attire for a classy place.

There was only one older couple to my left, sitting by the window, across from me, who left soon after. I ordered a prosciutto and cheese croissant and cappuccino.

Gondola Scene toward San Maggiore and Giudecca

The Florian Caffe

Lunch at Florian Caffe

As I waited for my food, I admired every inch of this amazing room, taking note of the detailed walls and ornate lighting and wondered if walls could talk, what would they say?

Then, came walking down the hallway toward me, was a strikingly, gorgeous beauty of a woman, in an immaculately tight fitting, low cut white lace dress, followed by a man twice her age. They came into my room and sat across from me in the corner. I was inspired immediately on how beautiful she was. The young woman had long dark brown hair that fell halfway down her bust. She could have been a model, with ancestry blend of Spanish, Asian or an Italian mix. I saw the lace of the low cut dress meet the tan line. I tried not to stare.

After a bit, I saw them trying to take a selfie photograph together and so, I offered my photographic services and asked, "Would you like me to take your picture?"

"That would be great, if you don't mind," the older man said.

"Sure," I said as he handed me his cellphone. I took a few snaps and then he asked, "Do you want me to take yours?"

"Yeah, sure," I said, handing him my phone. He took a few and one was a little soft, but good expression of me sitting there behind a table at the Florian. Later, many would say it was a great photo of me. More importantly, the photograph the man had taken of me, documented that I was truly there in Venice at the Florian Caffe.

Minutes later, after I finished my meal, the beautiful woman got up to refresh herself. Then, it hit me as she walked away. An opportunity and idea popped into my head. "Ok Marco, this is your chance," I said to myself. "You don't know unless you ask."

Me at the Florian Caffe

"Excuse me Sir. Would you mind if I photographed your lady friend?" I asked.

He looked at me and said, "That would be fine."

"Wow!" I thought to myself, "He said it's ok."

The woman came back and the man whispered to her before she sat down and nodded my way. She turned around and smiled, flattered and said, "Where do you want me?"

I responded quickly and said, "Right there," as I motioned to the opposite corner, close to the right of me. She sat down and struck a perfect pose. "She's done this before," I thought. I composed her with the paintings and frescoed walls and an ornate lamp above. Her vibrant red leather designer purse, snug to her side, matched her lip color. She looked amazing even before I snapped the shutter. The woman had an otherworldly beauty. It was perfect.

"God, is she beautiful," I unconsciously was thinking. "This is a real treat." First shot, "Click." Second shot, a slightly different expression, "Click." Then, I moved closer for a tighter crop, for a third and last shot. "Click." They were all great. Three photos in three minutes. It was a portfolio shot for sure.

"Thank you so much. Grazie!" I told her and acknowledging the man for the permission.

I handed the man my business card, and I asked for his, "Do you have a card and can I send you photos later?"

Without a word, he laid down a business card, and I took a photo of it.

"Thank you again," I said as I walked out. I couldn't believe what had just happened. It was a striking experience. This was the most beautiful woman I had seen in years, I got to photograph in a moments notice, in the most famous coffeehouse in all of Italy. It surely had been a miracle.

As I walked away, I began to stack up all the amazing experiences that were unfolding. The solo gondola tour just this morning. Now this amazing beauty at the Florian Caffe, where I had a five minute photo shoot, coming away with fantastic photos in a matter of a few short minutes. The evening before, getting a new cellphone and walking from one end of Venice to the other. The four bronze horses photographed on top of St. Mark's Basilica before that. The Doge Palace Tour, Bridge of Sighs and Murano Glass Factory, earlier that day. Before that, the train ride from Rome, and all the experiences in Rome itself; Castel Sant'Angelo, St. Peter's Basilica, The Sistine Chapel, The Colosseum. Piazza Navona, The Pantheon and Trevi Fountain. Now, I had a beautiful collection of photographs made.

All these events were now stacking up, with this last one being especially surprising and quick. It appeared that some kind of serendipity was rising.

After the Florian, I photographed the band outside and the square again and bought a few souvenirs.

"This has turned into another amazing day. Yesterday was an epic day. So was today. What were the chances of that?" I thought. "Somebody is orchestrating something, somewhere."

I took the vaporetto back up The Grand Canal to the Ferrovia stop, by Santa Lucia Train Station, only a few minutes from my hotel. Then I regrouped and was hungry for a great dinner.

Back at Hotel Abbazia, my friendly hotel clerk, Stefano, suggested Tre Archi, a great restaurant along Canal de Cannaregio, only a ten minute walk away.

I took a break, got freshened up and made a zig-zag walk to Tre Archi, making my way there by GPS on my trustworthy

Redmi 6A Italian cellphone. I had a fried Calamari and Polenta. It hit the spot.

By the time I was finished, it was dark. I was a little concerned about the walk back alone, through narrow streets and alleys at night. Again the GPS led me back. I said a small prayer for safety, and walked fast and sure, remembering nearly the way in which I came.

Then, I saw my street where my hotel was. I was now good. I settled into my room and previewed all my images. I was very happy on what I had captured with my camera and cellphone, but, that beauty at the Florian was over-the-top. I had captured a beauty and a miracle.

San Polo and the Last Day

My last day in Venice I wanted to check out the Rialto Fish Market by The Rialto Bridge in the San Polo District. This was a highlight activity for many seeing Venice for the first time. So, I thought I might catch some interesting photos and witness a top cultural spot, with the locals shopping for fresh fish.

After being dropped off at the Rialto Bridge dock, I walked across the main bridge area, which was double sided, inside and out. The inside walkway had shops on both sides, which was not visible from The Grand Canal, and walkways on the both exteriors, facing the canal.

The streets were cut up, non-grid like, leading to the fish market, so the GPS on the Italian phone led the way.

I came to the outdoor market area and the fish were laid out under awning roofs, highlighted by cheap lighting and handwritten signs. That was the first fish market area, one long strip. The main staff were four guys. They enjoyed selling, wheeling and dealing and waiting on customers. I photographed it up and down, with all different kinds of fish.

Across from this market was what looked like the more attractive market, inside a bricked arched canopy, with all the displays connected in the shape of a square. I missed seeing the sign that said, "No Photographs or Video." After I got some shots, I was making a sweeping video when a man got in my

The Rialto Bridge

Rialto Fish Market

face and said, "No Fotographica!" and pointed to the sign.

"Oh Crap. Damn!" I thought as I instantly felt awful for temporarily violating their photo policy, unaware. I thought it best for me to leave the area, so I did, feeling a bit shamed.

On the other side of this building was a cool scene with many boats docked on both sides of a medium sized canal. In all honesty, the fish market area fell flat for me photographically and otherwise. Although it was interesting to see this famous fish market, I tried to get something interesting captured, but it wasn't happening, so I moved on. In retrospect, I wish I would have spent my energy somewhere else. Any street in San Polo, or just getting lost again, would have been so much better.

I explored the area beyond the fish, following people to a main drag and to find one of only a handful of public restrooms in all of Venice. A street sign read: WC Toilette. There was a long, narrow alley street leading to the WC, and it was no more than seven feet wide. The light was interesting in this alley street, with flag fabrics hanging, draping its walls. It was good enough for a photograph, and I caught someone walking into my frame.

Coming back to the heart of San Polo's main street, Ruga Vecchia San Giovanni & Calle Cinque, I noticed a coffee shop on a corner that was filled with Moka Pots of every shape, size and color, in the display window. I thought this would be a great souvenir, something I could use to make stovetop coffee and it would always remind me of Venice.

As I walked in, I saw a store wide long counter filled with amazing deserts. I knew I had come to the right place. I ordered a cappuccino with a double shot, a pistachio cannoli and chocolate dipped cookie. I sat by the window, watching the people walk by. I took a photo of my desert and drink against the street outside the window. Enjoying my snack, I lingered in the shop to soak up the atmosphere. Before I left, I bought a pound of choice espresso beans and the single serving Bialetti Musa Moka Pot.

I had to watch my time, as the group gondola tour that was part of my package, was on for 6:00 p.m. I would need to be down at The Gritti Palace, not far from St. Mark's Square, in plenty of time before shoving off.

I went back to the hotel to regroup, then I remembered about customs, that you had to have every receipt of anything purchased, that you were bringing back home. Somehow, I didn't get a receipt for the moka pot and the beans, so I would have to take my moka pot and coffee back to Goppian Caffe in San Polo to get a receipt, then back on the vaporetto down to St. Mark's Square and get to the gondola tour leaving The Gritti Palace.

I made the return trip to Goppian Caffe by 4:00 p.m., then back to San Marco for the group gondola, arriving a bit early, getting in line about forty-five minutes before my last event on my last day in Venice. It was a bit of lost time, but it was ok because I got an extra roundtrip on the vaporetto up and down The Grand Canal that provided more great sights in wonderful weather.

The group gondola ride had ten boats on a string with a serenading singer and guitarist on one of the boats. It was five boats away, as we shoved off. It wasn't nearly as exciting as my solo gondola ride the day before, but it allowed for a few more scenes. We eventually heard the singer's voice bounce off the walls, once we entered a narrow canal. That was the fleeting high point.

Cappuccino and Cannoli in San Polo

Down the Grand Canal on Last Day

Me on the Group Gondola Ride

After this last gondola ride, I took one more gondola boat scene photograph back at St. Mark's Basin, and just as I was framing the shot, a huge cruise ship came in and parked out in the bay, blocking the whole view of San Giorgio Maggiore and Giudecca in the distance. I thought this was so wrong for this huge ship to be so close, cutting out the view of the historic landscape. I had heard later, that they would be outlawing cruise ships from docking there anymore. A ship that large displaces the water in the large canal and suddenly, Venice becomes overrun with masses of people all at once.

I took my last vaporetto home to the hotel and got wonderful, soft late afternoon light on all I could photograph on my last ride back on The Grand Canal.

My last dinner in Venice was Spaghetti Carbonara at a Cannaregio neighborhood cafe near the hotel. It was a great last meal.

I would need to get up early and be at the train station no later than 6:15 a.m. to shove off for Pescara, my grandfather's hometown region.

Venice had been spectacular in every way, more than I had originally imagined. The charm and ornate beauty, the romantic otherworldliness of life on the water, endless canals and bridges, narrow alleyways, surprises around every corner, being transported back into history, and the winged lion of St. Mark appearing everywhere, in statues, on doors, gondolas and on lampposts.

I would be leaving one part of my trip for a totally different part of my trip. In four days, I had received a generous overview, in the one city I had dreamed about more than any other. Now, I was eager to see where my ancestors came from.

Vaporetto on The Grand Canal

Last Ride on the Vaporetto

The Train to Pescara, Pt. II

The guys at the fabulous Hotel Abbazia, Stefano and Fabio, put together a bagged breakfast for me with those amazing chocolate croissants I had every morning, with some juice and other snacks. It was waiting for me at the front desk in a brown paper bag, for my train ride, being I had to leave so early. I thought that was really kind of them to think of me that way, on my way out. Because of that special service, I would stay there again in a heartbeat.

I had taken their photographs a few days earlier, to remind myself how great they had been, making my stay in Venice so memorable.

"Grazie! Molto Grazie!" I said as I left the hotel.

I walked out into the quiet, early morning, still black as night, down the narrow alley street outside the hotel, with not a soul around. Past the hotel, I rolled my two pieces of luggage down Calle Priuli dei Cavaletti, making a right onto the main drag, the Lista di Spagna, and strolled past the Scalzi Bridge and Scalzi Church. The three minute walk seemed much longer, as it was a bit spooky, walking the deserted streets of Venice, in the deserted early morning hour. As I walked up the steps to the Santa Lucia Train Station, carrying my two bags with my large messenger camera bag strapped around me, I finally mailed my postcards from Rome, in the mailbox right outside the Station.

I reached the platform at 6:15 a.m., and there was only one lady waiting. We struck up a short conversation to kill some time and the awkwardness of an empty train station with no one else around. I took a quick look at the departure/arrival screens above.

"Buon Giorno," I said.

"Buon Giorno," she replied.

"Where are you going?" I asked.

"Bologna. I have to go there to renew my license. I can't do it here. Then, I have to go South. You?"

"Pescara. It's the region where my grandfather came from," I said.

"Ok. Yes. Nice area."

As I viewed the track monitor screens, I found my train #8801 and its destination read, Lecce, a city in Italy's Southern Apulia region. It would be nearly a half hour before my departure track number would appear, getting tighter to my departure time of 6:55 a.m. That made me a bit nervous. I couldn't miss this train. This was where my a la carte part of my vacation began.

Finally, a half-hour later, the monitor read track 4. I was glad I didn't have to walk far. There were twenty tracks in all and I was close to where I needed to board.

"Ciao!" I said to my temporary friend and made it to my train car #7.

I noticed the vibe was different in second class. I got situated in my seat, 9D and the row was in the center of the car, near where the general luggage storage was, but there was plenty of room overhead, so I secured my two luggage bags above me. I just needed to keep an eye on my two pieces, from people coming and going.

A family boarded and settled twenty feet in front of me. They were loud with children, with one boy making a continual fuss about everything. I instantly saw the difference between first and second class. Quiet vs. loud. It was fine. I would only be riding second class on this train. My last two trains after Pescara would be first class again. I would arrive five hours earlier than planned. That was priceless. How much so, I had no idea.

The train got moving in less than ten minutes. They didn't mess around in Italy. Once boarded, trains take off quickly.

Somewhere outside of Rimini, before Ancona, I suddenly started writing. It was like an egg was breaking open, and something began to pour out and was unfolding in my mind.

I had wondered even before I left, if I would write about being in Italy. Now, here it came. I immediately wrote a passage that came complete, of what I might find there up ahead. Then, I fell asleep.

A stop at Rimini, along the Adriatic Coast

Reverie

I was drifting in and out of reverie on the train from Venice, recounting all that I experienced, on my life's greatest trip. The ride was smooth on the bullet train, where it didn't distract from my recollections. It was hard to believe all that I had seen in Rome and Venice. It had been a whirlwind over the last seven days in those two amazing cities. I was curled up with my new bag of memories, from my visits and the remarkable photographs I had made, with one of the coolest cameras I ever owned, my Sony Alpha 6300 mirrorless with a kit zoom, and two great lenses, a 35mm F1.8 and a 20mm F2.8. They were equivalent of a 52mm normal and a 30mm wide angle, with the high resolution cropped sensor type camera.

If I had seen nothing more than these two cities, what I had captured was a huge accomplishment in itself, but there would be so much more, going into a new leg of my trip. I was leaving a traditional trip, where everyday there was a picture making agenda, visiting all the top sites. Now, I was going into a deeper part of my trip, that somehow was hearkening back to my childhood with memories of an Italian family, and the feeling of my being Italian.

I was recollecting all my scenes captured, which gave me great joy. A dream had come true, with my camera. I would have images to work on for the rest of my life. There were hundreds, thousands even. As a professional photographer, classically trained in all aspects of still photography, I would know exactly how to work those images in many different ways, in post processing.

As I rode that train to Pescara, down the Adriatic coast, excitement filled me as if I was on my way to some enchanted place. It reminded me of driving in the car with my mom and dad and brothers, on our way to my grandma and grandpa's house on Sunday, for it was another enchanted place, where love hit us when we walked through the door, smothered in kisses from our aunts and grandma, and loving endearments from our uncles and grandpa, and hanging out, laughing and running around with our cousins. Walking onto that back porch, dried green beans and vegetables lined up on the right, with baskets for selling their farmed goods near the roadside, worked from the acre plus size garden, that started at the end of the backyard, and stretched as far as the eye could see, beyond the chicken coup.

I remembered the Italian air inside that home, with the antique photographs on the walls and the tables, the furniture and the ornate tablecloths and the smell of the amazing food made and long gone. A certain scent of an Italian household always remained. Nearly fifty years later, I would sense that Italian air again.

What would he find out when he got there, first to Pescara? Would he really be going to Moscufo? He wasn't sure how he would get there yet, and it was still up in the air, because before the train change in Venice, he wasn't going to Moscufo at all. There wouldn't have been enough time, only a day and a half. Marco had thought Pescara would have been close enough to his grandfather's hometown, because wouldn't it be a hassle to get there? Pescara was the place he always associated where his grandfather came from anyway. It wasn't until ten years ago that he learned that his grandfather really came from Moscufo, the commune town forty-five minutes inland. Something evolved, and he would be going there after all. Something waiting in Moscufo began to sink in. "There's something there. I'm not sure what it is, but I have a feeling," he thought to himself.

As the trip evolved, something else in my life was unfolding. I didn't know exactly what that was yet. My life would be changing because of this trip. It would carve out a new path when I returned home. But for now, I was on my way into the unraveling of a mystery. The mystery of our Italian family. Its beginning for us and how it had ended.

As I rode that train from Venice to my grandfather's hometown region, I studied the countryside outside the window, and how the terrain was beautiful with its different agricultural patterns and arrangements, the old crumbling structures, and the Italian graffiti littered walls of the train stations and its cars.

Now, he was traveling fast on a bullet train to Pescara, into the heart of it. His origin. It was up ahead, down the Adriatic coast.

Arrival Pescara

Soon, the TrenItalia train pulled into Pescara Centrale train station. Upon arrival, Marco was hungry and needed an espresso or cappuccino. It would depend on the place. Just inside the front door leading to the street, he saw a cafe bar and got one of those chocolate croissants he had everyday in Venice. The cappuccino was decent too.

"I needed that," he thought as he surveyed the area. After he was finished, he walked next door to a newsstand that had a few National Geographic Special Issues, Italian Edition, like "Speciale Archeologia La Roma," that was about the top monuments in Rome, on how they appeared pristine and functioned in their day, and how they remained today. Again, it was a reminder that he had chosen wisely, with two long visits at The Pantheon, that was highlighted in the edition. He had been drawn to it, and now was so grateful for the experience of all that was inside and outside, and the great photographs made, and that special Sunday mass in the round ancient building with the hole in the roof.

He rolled his luggage across the street, but overshot the hotel on the square, by a block, making his way back, due to the GPS not being totally accurate. It would be the Best Western Hotel Plaza on the Piazza del Sacro Cuore, on the square.

Upon checking in, he instinctively asked the hotel clerk about Moscufo. "Scusi, Can you tell me, is it difficult to get to Moscufo?"

"Oh, No…The bus goes everyday, from across the street, right over there," as he pointed out the door. Then, the clerk pulled up a bus schedule, as if from a magic hat, from below the counter. "Here's the schedule. The bus leaves from Pescara Centrale in the morning."

"Wow" I thought to myself. "He gave me the schedule, just like that."

This was peculiar. First the train change in Venice, allowing him to arrive five hours early. Now, the bus schedule laid out for Moscufo.

"This is meant to be in some way. It's too easy. I thought it would be much more difficult," Marco pondered.

"Grazie!" He thanked the clerk for the information and the bus schedule. It was settled there and then, that he'd be going to Moscufo tomorrow. It was like it had been pre-arranged.

When he got to his room, he felt a little queasy. He stopped and stood still, and then, felt the movement of the train, the swaying back and forth. Then he said, looking at the floor, "Why am I still moving? Oh no. Motion sickness. Crap." Then he thought, "No wonder. I was going backwards on the train at 100 mph for four hours. I will have to get something to tame this down."

He found a Farmacia a few blocks from the hotel. He wasn't grossly sick, but just enough to not be at his total best. Slightly dizzy and out of sorts.

"Scusi, do you have something for motion sickness?" He asked the main clerk. The man motioned to the English speaking technician.

"Yes?" She came walking over.

"Do you have something for motion sickness? I just got off the train and…I'm still moving," I said.

She went and got a box of tablets called "Geffer"- granulate effervescente, it said, like Alka-Selzer. She didn't realize what I needed was not just for my nausea. I needed something to calm the motion still happening. Then, he realized, "It will just have to wear off. Push through Marco." He went back to the hotel and took one tablet with a glass of water.

He came back out and decided to walk down by the seaside, to the water's edge, in this resort town. On the way, he saw a pizza place and needed some lunch. "Trieste Pizza," it said. Personal pan size was the only size they had. He sat at a table near the street. Another Margherita style pizza, but with sausage. It was delicious.

He felt something missing here. Something incomplete. Or, was it just boring compared to over the top Venice? How could any place compare with that?

It was mostly a fashion retail district with blocks of shops in section of Pescara where he was. "Surely, there is more to Pescara than this," he thought.

No, it was something else, not quite evident. He walked down to the Ponte del Mare bridge, that was shaped like an eel, that he had read about. An ultra modern bridge that looked out of place in Italy. It could have been from anywhere in America.

He walked up the ramp and got a good vantage view from the highest point, and saw the harbor and boats below.

"Am I missing something here? Is this it?" Marco said to himself.

He felt disappointed. Surely, there was something he wasn't seeing. He wouldn't have time to canvas all of Pescara in two

Pescara Cafe with Woman

days, being mostly on foot, and dizzy at that, from that 100 mph train ride that he rode backwards.

He took a few selfies from top of the bridge, with part of the town behind and below. Then, he thought about tomorrow. A surge went through him. It was excitement and importance at the same time. Then, it hit him.

"Now I get it. Pescara isn't supposed to be anything, like a destination. It's just a stop over for tomorrow. Hopefully by then, this motion sickness will have died down. I'll just take it easy today. After all, it's been a go, go, go for seven straight days. I can use a bit of a break."

"Tomorrow is Moscufo." He got a sense that it was a really big deal beyond the obvious. "I'm really going to Grandpa's hometown. Wow." After all this time, he was finally getting there. It would be a day like no other.

Something Waiting in Moscufo

After breakfast that morning, Marco walked over to Pescara Centrale bus station in front of the larger railway station, at the Piazza della Republica, to get ready to leave for Moscufo.

He had bought a ticket at one window, only to be told by another bus clerk that it was the wrong ticket, and was directed to another ticket counter, to buy the final roundtrip bus ticket. The ticket then read: Bigaliotto Suburbano, Tratta Sub, Euro: 2.40. 8/6/19 (June 8th).

There were three bus lanes where the buses lined up, but no indication which one was for Moscufo. "It took me three times to be directed to the right bus to board for Moscufo. When in doubt, ask more than once, surrounded by only Italian speaking people. Eventually, somebody tries to help you, and gets you where you need to go."

Finally, someone who understood English, saw my ticket and motioned to the right lane. "This one here," a man said.

"Grazie," I replied.

A few minutes later, the bus to Moscufo pulled up. The driver got out to have a break. I was eager and excited and got in line. Ten minutes later, the driver stood by the bus and motioned us on. As soon as you stepped up, you scanned your ticket and admission was granted. I sat behind the second door, about half way back. There was a pre-recorded announcement

Pescara Centrale Bus Station

and at the end of the string of beautiful sounding words, I heard "Moscufo." I took a few snaps of the lighted sign inside, at the front of the bus. It read, "Moscufo." After all, this was a landmark event. We started to roll.

"Oh Gosh. I'm on my way to Grandpa's town. This is a miracle," I thought. "Look how far I've come. All the way to Italy, and now to Grandpa's town. This is really something. The extra time I gained getting to Pescara early, allowed me to do this today. Not an accident at all," Marco thought as the bus pulled away.

He started filming when the bus swung in an arc past the Pescara Centrale Train Station. It was a forty-five minute ride on a noisy, rickety bus, that had great views on the way and the way back.

"I wonder what they must be thinking," he thought about the three of them, his grandma, grandpa and his father, as he took the bus ride over. He knew they were seeing this, watching it as it was unfolding. "I'm sure they're smiling, maybe even amazed, for this was rare. I am the first of the grandchildren to make it there."

Right before I was dropped off at the center of town, at Largo Garibaldi Piazza, on the main drag, we drove past the olive fields. My friend Tonio had told me that Moscufo had some of the finest olive oil in all of Italy. Later, upon returning to the states, I discovered that Moscufo and Pianella, where my grandfather was born, were two areas part of "The Golden Triangle," a top region in Italy for olive oil production.

I was dropped off on Via Aldo Moro at 10:16 a.m. As the bus drove away, I looked over the immediate area and took pictures of my first sights. Then, I walked up to the first string of buildings off the main street by a Farmacia. There was hardly a soul around, when a few minutes later, I approached someone who just came out of the Farmacia with a pharmacist. I asked them about the historic church, "Scusi, Can you you tell me where is the Chiesa, Abbey of Santa Maria del Lago?"

A man translated for me to the pharmacist, as only one spoke better English. "It's about two kilometers or so. Quite a ways," he said.

I thanked them and walked over to an inside group of buildings, that was the town's square called Piazza Umberto. It was shaped like an elongated oval, with a yellow decorated city municipal building, which was the City Hall, at one end, across from another church, with other old world buildings completing the oval. A design shaped like a fingernail covered the ground. Near me was a cafe.

"Oh Good. A cafe. I can get a much needed espresso and hit the toilette. The guy made my espresso while I used the restroom, that looked like it had been converted, with a close angled ceiling and odd light switch. I came back out and paid for my espresso that included an amazing chocolate dipped cookie, for only $.50 Euro. I sat at a small table and took a picture of it to savor the moment, making it a memory.

I didn't linger long, as time was ticking and I needed to get moving. I downed my coffee and cookie.

I walked out into the piazza and it became a special moment. I stood for minute looking at everything. I had to touch the ground and get a photograph of that, something I had dreamed about for a long time. I took a few selfies to get the best possible scene with the piazza background and me. I landed a good one.

"Wow. This is really it." Then I thought, "I wonder if they're seeing me here, my grandpa, my grandma and my father? Sure they are," I said to myself.

Piazza Umberto di Moscufo

Touching Ground in Moscufo

Cloud Over Piazza Umberto

Then, right after that selfie photograph of me touching the ground in the Moscufo square, I got a sense of something strong and peculiar overhead. I suddenly began to feel, the presence of my grandfather, my grandmother and my father. That feeling grew and I felt them close. Was I imagining this? No. In time, I would understand that their presence was real. This awareness would fade, not interfering with my picture making agenda.

I moved away from the cafe, walking up the incline toward the yellow City Hall building, inside the piazza oval, taking as many photos as possible, looking for what was the most attractive scene in front of me. Branching off the oval by the City Hall was a narrow alley type street, where I ended up finding my best scene.

A brick lined street, not more than ten feet wide, ended into a small courtyard, where a weathered building with many windows faced me, that had an arched doorway with a sculpted face above, and an ornate wall lamp hung above near my right. The light was still late morning and hitting the building favorably. Making this a black and white photograph, I moved in taking more shots, then saw the alignment I needed to make. I inched backwards a few feet until I framed the composition for its best version. The scene shouted, "Old World Moscufo!" and that image now proudly hangs on my black and white Italy wall. This was the one scene that captured that day best in Moscufo.

It was only 11:29 a.m. when I made that photograph, an hour after I arrived. I checked all that I shot, with a few good ones, and now this new one was under my belt. It was an accomplished scene.

I had to keep moving and watch the time for departure of my return bus back to Pescara. That was roughly only three hours away and I needed to make out it to the historic landmark church, the Abbey of Santa Maria del Lago. It was tops of the remaining bucket list. Somehow, I had to make it there.

The Moscufo brochure Tonio had given me nearly seven years ago, in his home, had details of that church I remembered. I would get there at all costs, even if I had to walk.

It was two kilometers away and I was all alone in a sparsely populated Italian village with hardly anyone around, and the people I did meet, didn't speak much English. In most ways, I was on my own.

I came back out to the same main street where the bus had dropped me off. I took a video of an immediate group of interesting shaped buildings, and walked across to an overlook where I took a sweeping video of the beautiful valley below of Moscufo. I commented as I filmed, "I just landed in Moscufo, about an hour ago, up the street there, and this looks like it's going to be an amazing visit. Because, if you look out here, I just discovered this, is an amazing panorama view of the area. What beautiful countryside. Moscufo, Italy, where Alonso Conte, Sr. came from in 1911, at sixteen years old, with twenty-five dollars. I had an amazing espresso already. I'm going to try to go find the Santa Maria de Lago church. It's supposed to be a high point of this town. Alright!"

Old World Moscufo

I had walked out beyond the piazza square and down a main road, feeling my way. Along the way, I made another photo, of a mound of trees on a hilltop in the distance, framed by trees in the foreground. An Italian countryside scene.

I kept walking, then I came to a fork in the road with another church in the middle. I took the left fork via Michelangelo street, and came upon some rustic, old buildings that looked like homes. Across the street was what looked like an Italian outdoor oven, but ended up being a burial memorial. I didn't see anyone around to ask if it was ok to photograph, when a small dog came barking across the street. He looked harmless, just protecting his turf.

"Hi there buddy!" I said, trying to make friends. An older lady came out of the house, yelling to the dog from across the street,

"Basta! Basta!" I knew that meant "Enough!" I waved and motioned my camera to the monument. She nodded "Ok," and I gave another wave. "Grazie," I shouted to her across the street.

I took a few pictures, but here was an opportunity to ask how to get to the most well known church.

"Scusi. Chiesa Santa Maria del Lago?" I asked.

Her husband appeared and wranged their dog back to the house. He came over and I asked again, "Scusi, Ciao. Chiesa Santa Maria del Lago?"

"Eh, You drive?" He asked, motioning with his hands, barely speaking English.

"No, I'm walking," I said, picking up my feet illustrating a march.

His wife across the street motioned to him, pointing ahead to his car parked on the street, and blurted something that must have been, "Take him!"

Moscufo Hilltop Countryside

The man, motioned to the car, as we walked over to it. I felt at ease with no hesitation.

"Grazie," I said as we both got in. Before we pulled away, I instinctively asked him, "Do you know Tonio Arzuri?" And he said, "Oh Tonio! Si Tonio!" I thought that was interesting, but didn't know if he really understood me.

We pulled away and he drove me down a long road past a small town business district that was part rural. I didn't realize it at the time, but we drove past the olive fields on our left, that I would examine closer on my walk back. My new old timer friend was driving me to the church, saving me valuable time.

I began filming and making commentary, after we pulled away, as if I was on some documentary assignment:

"Something incredible just happened. I just met a met a friend on the street, who knows Tonio, who's from Moscufo, and this man knows him. And, I'm wanting to go to the church, which is the Santa Maria del Lago, and it's quite a walk, and this fine gentleman who understood what I wanted to do, is driving me there. I think that's pretty remarkable." Suddenly, we drove into the driveway of the church. "So, uh…We are here! Amazing," I said as I finished my video.

Everything appeared to be falling into place, the photographs I needed to make and the locations I needed to visit, all within a specific time frame. This was another miracle.

When we came to a stop in the church parking lot, the front of the church looked just like it had in the brochure Tonio had given me seven years ago. How is it I ran into this guy and he drove me where I needed to go, and did he really know Tonio? It started becoming more peculiar as the day wore on.

I got out of the car and offered to pay him for his trouble but he refused to take any money. The sign of a good man.

I took a photo of him in the car, in the driveway, with the church in the background. I wanted to remember this moment on this day in my grandfather's hometown. I took a short video clip as well and said, "Say Hi Tonio."

He said, "Tonio, Tonio. Paolo. Paolo!"

Months later, I would ask Tonio when he got back from his own trip, to see if he really knew this man named Paolo from Moscufo. He did. On Tonio's trip right after mine, Paolo had told Tonio that he had driven me to the Santa Maria del Lago church. Halfway around the world, a man I had met in my grandfather's hometown, had known my new uncle friend Tonio, who I had met in the appliance showroom, in the big box home improvement store, seven years earlier in Columbus, Ohio. What a small world it is.

"Grazie!" I said, as he drove away, dropping me off at the church.

I photographed the church front and its signs, and a large cross out front. It was now past noon and the light was not at its best. I tried to see if the church was open, but the front doors were locked.

Walking around the back, was a much better scene. Medieval brickwork and windows with border carvings, and the light looked much lower than it had been out front. I started snapping away. If nothing else, this scene would work and be a salvageable souvenir record of my visit.

I worked the scene at the back of the church for a good ten minutes, shooting a variety of the three cylinder shapes making up the rear of the church, zooming into just one of the ornate bordered windows that was lined with carvings of animals.

I went looking for an office or someone on site, past an outdoor mausoleum, but there was no one. I returned to the

Santa Maria del Lago Church, rear view

back of the church, and made my best photographs of Santa Maria del Lago. I reviewed my photos and was happy with my scenes captured, although a bit disappointed that I would miss seeing the church's interior. There had been no time to find out if it would have been open before my arrival in Moscufo.

I wasn't even sure I was going make it to this town at all. Remember? The train change from Venice, gave me the extra time in Pescara, that made this day possible.

I was grateful that I had captured The Piazza Umberto, the selfie of me touching the ground, the "Old World Moscufo" scene, the Moscufo countryside hill shot, and now, the back of the historic landmark church. If I shot nothing else in Moscufo, I'd be happy.

I knew my walk back would be quite a huff, but that was ok. I got my shots. I just would need to make it to this other church where my departure point was around 3:25 p.m.

I walked along the side of the road, after leaving the church, and here I was all alone by myself in this small commune town, not knowing where I was really going, but had a general sense of direction on the walk back, and I had felt God protecting me. I had felt those three near me, that whole afternoon, that of my grandfather, my grandmother and my father.

So far, it had been a surreal but wonderful day with much accomplished, with sights and locations seen and photographs made.

Up ahead, off the right side of the road were the olive fields. Suddenly, there was another scene presented to me, on a dirt road leading to a building, an old ornate house, with the driveway lined with olive groves on both sides. I had to get the shot, even though I might not have been allowed. I made some quick photos of the scene in color and black and white.

Santa Maria del Lago Church, detail

Back on the road, I came to a row of houses on the right. I needed someone's help again, getting me where I needed to go. I saw an attractive couple getting ready to leave in their car when I imposed on them.

"Scusi, I am needing to get to bus stop to Pescara," showing them my bus schedule, which had the name of another church as the departure point.

They tried to communicate with me, and were very friendly, but they didn't understand me at first, but I felt at ease and comfortable with them when, they motioned and said, "Get inside. We take you."

"Oh Gosh. This is happening again," I thought to myself. "A ride to where I need to go, just in time to get back to Pescara. Another miracle for sure."

I said a quick prayer, "God, Is this ok?" It felt right, so I got in the car and thanked them, "Grazie. Molto Grazie."

There weren't many roads in Moscufo, and this one main street made a loop. While we were driving, I instinctively asked, "Do you know Tonio Arzuri?"

"Oh Tonio! Si! Mia Madre and Tonio Madre - migliori amici," the vivacious woman said as we drove up ahead. I was thinking that she might have meant that, her mother and Tonio's mother were best friends.

"They can't possibly know Tonio too?" I thought. "Who knows? I'll take their photo before I get off."

They stopped at my original drop off on Via Aldo Moro, and I said, "Oh, No. Chiesi" and pointed to my bus schedule that showed the bus stop by another church's name, Chiesa Madonna Della Pieta. They understood and started driving again. I was hoping that they would get me there ok. Then, I saw the church, The Madonna Della Pieta.

Moscufo Olive Trees

We came to a halt and I got out. I asked for a photo. They posed graciously, showing my business card, but I forgot to ask for their names. Darn. I was too preoccupied with getting back to Pescara by way of the bus.

I thought it was very peculiar, that two friendly sets of strangers, in an Italian village, half-way around the world, both said they knew my friend Tonio from Moscufo, who I met in Columbus seven years ago, and they both drove me that afternoon to where I needed to go. What were the chances of that happening?

I walked down to the bus stop, which happened to be on the other side of the fork in the road where I originally met Paolo and his wife and their dog. Now, I was at the bus stop a good forty-five minutes early, but it was better to be early than late. If I missed this one, it would be hours before another bus came by, and probably in the dark.

The bus was on time and it was a great ride back, with more views of the Moscufo countryside. I shot another video clip showing all those olive fields again. Forty-five minutes later, I arrived back at the Pescara bus station at 15:40 p.m.

Back in Pescara, outside the hotel, was an interesting three-sided phone booth that looked both vintage and futuristic, I had shot the night before. This time in different light, I photographed it again before getting back to my room. It was worth a few more shots.

Without realizing how worn out I was, I passed out on the bed and had a great nap of indeterminate time.

The Violinista in the Square

I woke up to strikingly, beautiful music I heard coming from below. Was I dreaming? It sounded like a string quartet coming from the hotel lobby. Instinctively, I swung open my hotel room window and heard the music coming from a violinist playing somewhere outside in the square below, very sharp and clear.

I filmed it immediately, to capture the sound, because I couldn't believe what I was hearing. What was playing brought me to tears. It was my favorite song by soundtrack composer Ennio Morricone, the theme track to "Once Upon A Time In The West," and the song spoke to me like never before, in some strange but remarkable way.

What was going on? Something was. It wasn't just a song playing. It was a song playing just for me.

"I can't believe what I'm hearing," I said in tears, waking up from a nap. "Ennio Morricone. Ennio Morricone. 'Once Upon A Time In the West'. God knows that's my favorite music right now." I was choked up and could barely get the words out.

Then it hit me, "Oh God. You knew today was one of the most important days of my life, with the epic day in Moscufo, my grandfather's hometown. Yet, you weren't done with my day, and you gave me this song, in addition to the miracles I encountered in Moscufo. I don't know what to say, other than, Thank you, for what has been the most amazing day!"

It's my last day here in an Italian city. I'm overwhelmed with joy, but, "There's something else now, isn't there?" Marco asked God silently, when his accurate intuition kicked in. Something else began to unfold. It was no accident getting to Moscufo.

He grabbed his camera and raced down to the square below, approaching the violinist in the distance, hoping for another play of Morricone. He would want to be front and center, if he could get him to play it again.

There were many people out, strolling the square on a Saturday night. A guy passing by, with no inhibitions, nonchalantly stopped and joined in, singing along to the violin, pretending to be an unabashed Caruso.

I snapped pictures of Alessio, who was an older, long gray haired, classically trained violinist, playing an electric hollow body violin, connected to a great sound system.

I let him get used to me taking pictures of his performance, but first, I dropped a five dollar Euro bill into his hat, noticing he saw that.

A young twenty-something woman dropped by to talk to Alessio, who was between songs, taking a break. They spoke and laughed, and it seemed like they hadn't seen each other in awhile. They seemed very friendly. "Was she a lover?" I wondered.

Then, there was a break and I walked up and asked, hoping to hear the amazing piece again.

"Scusi, Can you play Morricone again?" I was hoping he knew I meant the same song. He nodded a "Yes" with a warm smile. I quickly got into position as I saw him reach for his bow, and this was starting like now, so I got ready on his right side, and as he started, I began filming him playing, moving in an arc

Violinist Alessio Playing Morricone

in front of him, ending on his left, with the Pescara train station in the distance behind him, as the music was ending.

He came to a gentle close of the last notes from "Once Upon A Time In The West," and he looked over at me. I teared up a second time. I didn't understand why this was affecting me so deeply.

"Thank you. Thank you very much," I said. Tears in my words.

All I could think of was, "God touched my life today, with the most amazing visit to my grandfather's hometown in Moscufo, Italy. Amazing photos and videos had been captured there. People who I never knew befriended me, each taking me where I needed to go, first by the dear, generous man, Paolo, to the Abbey of Santa Maria del Lago church, for photos. Then, I was taken to my last stop, for the bus, by a friendly couple, and they too acknowledged that they knew my friend Tonio back in Columbus, Ohio. Then, the most beautiful song in my life, played in the square, seemingly just for me, as I was waking up from a nap.

"Why did it make me cry, the song, 'Once Upon A Time In The West' by Morricone? Why did it bring me to tears, twice? There's something about that. Not sure what, but something."

It meant something alright.

The song had a different meaning, after hearing it in Pescara that afternoon, after Moscufo. It would always be a reminder of that epic day where Marco came face to face with his Italian culture of fifty years ago. The Italian culture that had been torn from his life.

Then, The Church of the Sacred Heart, at the Piazza Sacro Cuore square, would be his last photo taken in Pescara, the last of an Italian city on his trip, with the last light of the day.

The rest of that Saturday evening, he strolled by the seaside, having his last margherita pizza, and for desert his last gelato, same as the first one in Rome, chocolate and pistachio.

Tomorrow, would be the way back to Rome, all day on trains. He was still reeling when he turned in, taking stock of his most magnificent day, filled with more photographs. How that day and this trip, would change his life forever.

Church of the Sacred Heart, Pescara

Three Trains Back to Rome

My last day in Italy was spent entirely on trains. There was no direct route back to Rome from Pescara, so the first of the two trains would take me south to Foggia. There, I would transfer for the second train, a Northwest bound train for Rome. Then, it would be a shorter forty-five minute transfer train from Rome Termini train station to Rome Airport. Lastly, I would have to catch a shuttle from the airport to the hotel near Rome Airport for the last night. I would return back to the airport the following morning via shuttle for my flight back to the US.

It was great to see large areas of the Italian countryside again, but more than anything, it was a full day of reflection.

The first train from Pescara to Foggia, was the kind of European train I always wanted to experience, the kind with the outside hallways and closed off cabins, that conjured up many movie scenes, where people sat across from each other, either forcing communication or being indifferent. It excited me that I would finally get to experience this kind of train, on my last day in Italy.

It would take about two hours to reach Foggia. I had two passengers in my train cabin. An attractive, middle aged blonde with ponytail and nice figure, who sat directly across from me, and that was Claudia. On her side, a seat away, was a stout man named Giorgio. They spoke Italian well enough with each other back and forth.

I saw them glance my way occasionally, probably wondering what my story was, while I wondered about theirs.

At some point, the woman asked me my name and where I was going, I had figured from the little Italian I did know.

"Marco," I answered.

"Rome!"

She smiled. I asked her name,

"Come Si Chiama?"

"Claudia," she said with a twinkle in her eye. Our first exchange broke the ice. I asked a few questions with my Italian English app. She was intrigued on how well the app translated from our spoken voices.

She started asking me questions, talking into the phone, "di dove sei?" The translation app responded with "Where are you from?"

"USA, Columbus, Ohio," I said.

We carried on for a few minutes, communicating with the translation app, and we both laughed on how well it worked. It made me realize how much I understood Italian.

I told her, "I hope to learn Italiano when I get home."

"Bene, Bene," She said.

The old man on her side just watched from time to time, but Claudia and I had broken the ice. It was nice I had made a friend on my first train back to Rome.

We both retreated to our own space and I studied the outdoor terrain again from my window seat. It was so beautiful. The train showed yet more Italian delights; the Adriatic seaside, more interesting landscapes, train stations and oddities of buildings. Then, it began sinking in. Something had happened to me back there in Moscufo and Pescara. Something that resonated. As I watched the land and houses roll by in the Italian countryside, I realized something Big happened to me, mostly yesterday in my grandfather's hometown, but also had accumulated gradually all along in Rome and Venice. The totality of this trip was immeasurable on how it had changed me.

God had let Italy give me back something. They had worked it out together. It was the nudge and tap on the shoulder I felt back in Moscufo, that told me I had something to write about. It would not be easy, to take that train ride back to my youth. It had been a long and dark tunnel of pain.

I began asking myself, while the countryside was zooming by, "What is going on?" That was the question for my intuition that was 99% accurate most of the time. It was part prayer too. Intuition and prayer mixed together.

"Ok God...What are you trying to tell me? If you're trying to slowly tell me something, let me know what it is, but I'm afraid to ask."

Before the answer came through, I knew it had to do with my childhood, and what had happened to us, my brothers and I. But, this was about what had happened to me, because I had position in our family as second oldest, aware of many things in my surroundings, most of my life, recording all the events with reasonably good memory, long before I realized how acute my recording mechanism really was.

I was too restless to listen to my iPod shuffle, that had fifteen albums on it, enough for this trip. I liked the sound and the feel of the train instead. When would I ever hear or feel it again?

A few hours went by, and we were getting close to Foggia, a town in Southern Italy. I began looking at my boarding pass and

Last Train along the Adriatic Sea

saw it would be a short window to make my transfer train back to Rome, and I couldn't miss it. That gave me a touch of anxiety.

As Claudia and I and the other fellow Giorgio got ready to exit down the hallway, I showed her my connecting paper boarding pass and could she ask the conductor what track my upcoming train would be located, as we neared the doorway. The dispatcher called ahead after seeing my boarding pass, and was able to get the track number for me, and told me, "Don't worry. I'll show you."

"Oh Good," I thought, because I only had twenty minutes to make the connection.

God continued to put people in my path, when and where I needed it, and there was always great comfort in that.

Minutes later, we had disembarked from the train and the conductor motioned to me, as I said, "Ciao!" to Claudia. "Pretty woman," I thought again to myself. The conductor led me over to another track and pointed to the steps of the exact car I needed to board, and then said, "There!" A great samaritan. "Molto Grazie" I replied. I double checked my boarding pass info and stepped up into train carriage #1 of #8314.

We were back to coach style bullet train. I walked down the aisle and found my seat location by a window on the right, seat #10A. On my side was a single row of seats. On the left side was a double row. A few minutes later, a woman sat down right across from me and smiled. She was a smart looking brunette with a whimsical, care free vibe. Her name was Sofia.

We started rolling about 2:20 p.m. and now my second longest train for my last day in Italy was bound for Rome. It would be a longer train, about three hours.

Before long, the train attendants were coming by with a cart and gave out cookie snacks, coffee and drinks.

Sofia and I had introduced ourselves and she was trained as an attorney but worked in a corporate position, for which she was traveling to Rome for training. She was from Bari, at the foot of the boot. We had hit it off pretty well from the start of the train and the atmosphere was comfortable across from her.

I was about to have my cookie, reaching to tear the wrapper, when suddenly, Sofia whipped out a large piece of Focaccia pizza bread from her bag. I laughed immediately and said, "Do you always carry a large piece of Focaccia bread in your bag?" She laughed and said, "Do you want one?"

"If you're offering, Sure!" I said. And so, she pulled out another one. I had to take a photograph of it, as it hit my funny bone, and when I took the picture, I got a thumbs up from her, with a smile and the beautiful focaccia bread in the foreground perfectly framed for a lasting photograph. My second train friend had given me this memorable experience. We both chuckled and she remarked, "Bari has the best focaccia bread in all of Italy."

"Wow, Nice. Grazie!" I replied.

That gift of bread was the icebreaker from my second back-to-Rome train friend.

It seemed like wherever I went on my trip in Italy, people were there to give me a warm welcome, even as I was on my way out, leaving.

We made it to the Roma Termini at 5:20 p.m. I would now have an even shorter window connection time to catch my shuttle train to Rome Airport - Fiumicino Aeroporto, connecting in only fifteen minutes.

I asked Sofia the direction of the shuttle train, and she pointed to the other side of the platform. I would just have to watch for train #3326 to come by.

Focaccia Bread and Thumbs Up

"Grazie Sofia! Ciao!" I said as we went our separate ways.

The shuttle train at Roma Termini came by after ten minutes and I boarded with my two rolling bags. It reminded me more of a New York City subway. Standing room only. Now, I was getting tired. It had been a total of six hours on two trains through the Italian countryside, a long way back to Rome, and I still had a ways to go.

We got moving and it was a forty-five minute ride. When I got out, I made my way outside to the front of the airport. My next and last connection was the shuttle back to my last hotel, a few miles from Rome Airport. Now, I had a new problem. After seven hours, I just wanted to get to the hotel.

The Italian phone I had bought in Venice had no direct local calling service, only email, GPS, internet and limited texting. I had to notify the hotel that I needed picked up from Rome Airport. After trying to send an email that was unsuccessful in contacting the hotel, I ended up asking a young woman outside the airport near me, if she could call my hotel for a shuttle pick up. She got through and let me speak to the hotel front desk. Finally, they said, "Yes, Mr. Conte, we have your reservation. Our shuttle will be by in twenty minutes. It will be fine. We'll pick you up."

"Grazie," I said to the hotel clerk.

When I hung up, I gave the phone back to the woman and told her, "Grazie, Thank you!"

It was stressful, this last connection, because I was tired and hungry and I wanted this day to be done. After traveling all day on trains, I was exhausted. Over seven hours on three trains had been enough. It was approaching 7:45 p.m. and it was becoming, after all the traveling, the most stressful part of my last day.

As I waited for the shuttle, I saw in the middle parking lane, across from my curb, what looked like various shuttle buses lining up. I realized I needed to be over there and I asked which one was for Best Western Rome Airport.

After I walked over, "Scusi," I called to a man loading people up. "Best Western?"

He shook his head "No."

I saw another bus with a driver loading people up. "Best Western?" He said, "Yes" and pointed to getting on. He took my bags and loaded them in the back. I double checked the lighted sign on the front and it said, "Best Western Rome Airport." When I got in, I double checked once more and asked, "Best Western Rome Airport?"

"Yes," a man across from me said. I was losing my energy and patience, and I had been routed wrongly before. I couldn't afford that now. I needed the hotel.

When you're traveling alone, it's harder, all the way around. There are benefits. You can come and go as you please, and go see exactly what you want to see, when you want, not restricted to the consideration of another. When it comes to directions and navigation, you have to double-check, triple-check, when it's new terrain.

Ten minutes later, we were on our way to the hotel, my last one, not far from the airport, in an older part of town. My last night in Rome had finally come.

What a day! It had been great traveling on the two trains, both first class, with those colorful characters near me. But, by the end, I was trashed. I needed dinner and wanted to be settled, so I could relax. It got a bit hairy, getting that shuttle, but I made it. We pulled into the hotel.

I got checked in and got to my small, business size hotel room, where everything had been cut to half size. Single bed, small desk and bureau, 30" TV.

When I saw the bathroom, I laughed. "What in the world? How do you use anything without bumping into everything?" I said out loud to myself.

I had to take a picture of it. I couldn't believe how compact and close together all the bathroom pieces were. The toilet, the bidet, the sink and the shower drain with the curtain closing off the corner, were all within a foot or less of each other. It was sink and toilet on the North, the bidet on the East and shower on the South. Just make a quarter turn and you're there.

It was by far, the wackiest hotel on my whole trip. It didn't matter. I just needed a place to hang my head, a last stopover for the night. I would be leaving in the morning.

I freshened up quickly and made it downstairs in time for a late dinner. It was now pushing nine o'clock.

Finally, unwinding…

A waiter came by and I ordered a plate of pasta with red sauce, a salad and bread. No need for a menu.

The food came quickly and hit the spot after a long, trying day. Soon after, I felt restored, then I retired.

Leaving Rome

The next morning after check out, and coffee from a coffee cart, about a dozen of us loaded up the shuttle and made it out to the airport.

I had never been through customs like this, where we were snaked through various checkpoints and then got in line for individual kiosks. They each had their own scale for checked bags. You answered a few questions, scanned your passport, tagged your bag and dropped it off. Then, at another checkpoint, you scanned your passport again and the gate would let you through, only mine was blocked. They had agents standing by to assist you if you had any problems. Here, my passport photo with my corrective lenses off, didn't jive with the camera photographing me with my glasses on. So, off came my glasses, then it let me through. I thought that procedure needed some retooling. Who decided that anyway?

My large bag had been checked and I felt lighter with just my carry on, still on wheels, and my messenger camera bag loaded with all my precious photo gear.

After the security checkpoints, I came into a cluster of retail shops, where I bought some last minute souvenirs, like a coffee mug and small journal books, one with an old age Pantheon scene. A tourist trap. I stuffed and padded them inside my carry on bag.

As I was on my last walk to my gate, I heard a general announcement in Italian, very loud and clear, so I decided to record this as an Italian memory snapshot with my smartphone digital recorder app.

At a food court near my gate, I had my last great meal in Rome. It was suprisingly good. A thick, artisan French loaf with prosciutto and swiss, a chocolate croissant like I had every morning in Venice and a cappuccino. I photographed the last meal for my memories, like I had done for most of my meals.

"When will I ever make it here again?" I thought. "Someday I hope. Please let it be." A moment of sadness crept in.

Finally, I was now at my gate, ready for my flight bound for Chicago.

All my days, all my scenes, rushed through me, and I had surely been blessed by my life's greatest adventure, in the land I had so much longed to love and touch. I was reeling. Before long, I would be flying over the Atlantic, taking home too many gifts to catalog in my heart, mind and soul. So much had happened, yet the depth of my journey wasn't over. Another part of it was just beginning.

Post Italy Revelation

Returning to Columbus, a sardine can had been opened. It had all come together. The deeper meaning of a trip of a lifetime, the deeper meaning of a soundtrack song. Marco now saw the connection, possibly the other reason why the song brought him to tears. He saw a parallel.

In the movie, "Once Upon A Time In The West," the beautiful soundtrack music told half the story. The story about an Italian bride brought to The American West, only to lose her entire family, murdered by bandits, leaving the woman with heartbreaking loss.

The song's soaring vocals in crescendo, cried out the loss, a loss that Marco knew his whole life, all too well. He and his four brothers and their mom, all knew far too well. How their lives also, were forever changed. How that song played for their loss too, just the same.

The soundtrack song by Ennio Morricone now had greater resonance upon his return home. There were great miracles that happened for ten days in Italy. But, it was on the ninth day, his last day in Pescara, and more specifically, that afternoon in Moscufo, his grandfather's hometown, that it all changed.

His lifetime anguish of losing his father, and losing his Italian culture, that went with it, while still a child, that was the deepest part on why Italy drew him to itself. After all these years, God would return The Italian culture to Marco, that had been lost for nearly fifty years.

The song played the story of an Italian tragedy, both in a movie, but also for Marco, who traveled alone, in search of all things Italian, that he had loved so much, but had missed this deepest connection, most of his life.

In the car that morning, on his way to work…

"I put the music on again to 'Once Upon A Time In The West,' since I've been back, and instantly I'm struck. The music and melody rings right through me, like a big bell, and I immediately want to cry…and I don't understand why. It's happened ever since I returned that day from Moscufo, and I heard that song in a particular way, later back at the hotel on that afternoon in the square in Pescara. I woke up from a nap, that seemed like a dream I was in the middle of, a soundtrack. The soundtrack of my life."

"Why is this music doing this to me? What's the reason?" He said to himself.

He remembered the movie. A tragedy. The woman sings with a voice that soars with sorrow. She sings with beautiful sadness, the Italian bride who loses her family, murdered by outlaws, shortly after she arrives from Italy. She has to start over, from what was robbed of her. A new life in the American West.

"From what was robbed from her. Hmmm. For whatever reason, somebody wants me to look at this. This part of my life," Marco thought.

The music is a connection that rings from a parallel. The soundtrack song connects tragedy in a move to tragedy in real life, his life. The loss of his Italian father at too young an age, for he and his brothers and their mother. Their lives would never be the same. They too, would have to start over with much less than before.

The woman's voice soars, ringing the tragedy. A beautiful sadness.

Now, decades later, a dream fulfilled that connects him to his family's ancestry, while also giving him the greatest gift, a reason for the photographs, the most incredible trip of his life. He would bring back home, beautiful images to remind him of all he had captured. How he would never be the same. How all the elements came together, to speak to him that day in Moscufo, and shortly after, in the square below in Pescara, from his hotel room, a few hours after Moscufo. How a violinist played a perfect version of "Once Upon A Time In The West" soundtrack score. What were the chances of that happening?

The music made him explore why it was moving him this way, after all this time. He had heard it many times before, but it never affected him like this, until now. Then, he saw the tragedy and how the music expressed it so perfectly, for the movie and how the music was now speaking to him, about his life.

It was a connection deeper than he would realize. Did he need to look at it again? Others would bury a tragedy. He had moved on from his. Now, it bubbled up again, to show where he had come from, and how that ancestry ran deep and strong.

There was something else. Another layer on what Marco received upon taking that leap of faith to travel to Italy alone. Instinctively he knew, that he had to go alone. Despite the landing in Rome, Venice, Pescara and Moscufo, there was something more important than his ancestry. It was the greatest gift he had ever received, at this point in his life, because this trip became his life's greatest photo assignment. The core of who he was now, tied to the core of his ancestry, gave him his life's greatest joy with his camera. God knew how much he needed this. And images to bring back home? There were so many, he staggered on wading through the boatloads he was still sifting through, over a month later.

When he opened the hotel window to the square in Pescara that afternoon, after his visit to Moscufo, he immediately cried, hearing the music below, because it was one of the most beautiful songs in his life now, but hearing it was like God telling him, giving him his life's greatest gift, saying, "I know you love this song, and after all you experienced today in Moscufo, and in Venice and Rome, I wanted you to know, I wasn't done with your day. So, here's a little something else, to let you know how much I care for you."

With that music, Marco had cried, because he realized, God was giving him the desires of his heart that day, but also for ten days in Italy. The trip had been the greatest gift of his life, from where he was now.

It was a Big Deal, that he had gone on this trip by himself. He had never known anyone who had traveled to another country by themselves before. Marco wasn't exactly sure how it was going to go, traveling so far into the unknown, into the Italy he had longed for so many years. Everything had lined up for a trip to be as organized as well as it was. The travel lady he had met on the job a few years back, helped make it possible, as she taught him how the tour would go with its accommodations and built-in inter-connections.

It had been a serendipitous day in Moscufo, with just enough to photograph to bring back home. Photographs he made with just the right amount of sunlight on the back of the historic landmark church, The Abbey of Santa Maria del Lago, that had been locked up out front. The rear building windows had unique carvings, animals of some sort in hieroglyphic style on the stone borders around the windows. The roof border had castle like edging.

He had the courage to travel alone so very far away. Even with his love of all things Italian, he was still going into a foreign land, into the unknown. With the locations he had mapped out in Rome and Venice, he had a daily plan for photographs to make. He was imprinting the scenes into his heart, mind and soul, memories for a lifetime, to bring back home.

Instead of an open sardine can that revealed new information about his trip, it was more like a flower that kept on unfolding, releasing more and more pollen of memories from long ago.

Mission Fotographica

He had been back five weeks and when he started really looking at all the photographs he had taken, he couldn't believe how much ground he had covered in such a short time.

Marco had clearly been on a mission to prove that he still "had it." The ability to make great photographs again after all these years.

His abilities had turned back on for this trip, being in that special zone that was his alone, amongst the sea of people he encountered in Rome, first at Castel Sant'Angelo, then in St. Peter's Square, on the next day for the tour at The Vatican, The Colosseum, Piazza Navona and Trevi Fountain. Then, he found on his last day in Rome, a way to get no people in a photograph, on what became his favorite place of all, of ancient Rome undisturbed, The Pantheon.

Venice was even more crowded in spots, like St. Mark's Square. He found a way to incorporate the people into the photographs, then, just like in Rome, eliminate them, like up on the balcony of St. Mark's Basilica, with the Four Bronze Horses, shooting upwards toward the sky, with one horse's hoof prominently enlarged and galloping, closer to the camera with the wide angle lens, and the bell tower leaning in from the right, almost touching, compressing enough to complete the scene.

Or, a quiet, small alley street (Calle), showing how beautifully dense the city on the water was. So many bridges and canals, much of the time overrun with mobs of people, but then the serene scenes would appear, like the solitary gondolier, flowing through the narrow canals with no one else but the soft muted colors on the buildings, timeless scenes of yesteryear's dreams. Or, on the lost walk back home, along Rio Marin, captured with still reflection of water, and not a soul around.

God showed him, as the days grew into his trip, that it was becoming more special as time rolled on, with the surprises becoming more frequent.

God showed him, what was possible on this trip, and for his life. He took that leap of faith, and the surprises that were shown, he would never forget.

Days later, the memories of Italy were becoming more like someone else's life, not his own. He was astounded he had even gone.

"You got me to Italy," he said to God above. "You got me there in the most amazing of ways. I have to think that there's something else that goes with it, beyond the trip itself. Somehow, it has to mean a new beginning. A beginning of what's possible now that I'm back. Too much happened over there, that showed that God was with me, where I was by myself in Italy. I had to go it alone. A test of sorts. Could I go and it really be a great time?"

"It ended up being the greatest time of my life, where I was a spectator, a recorder of magical moments, a listener of beautiful sounds and language, an artist participant in a wondrous land. I achieved great success by making many images to bring back home, more than I could have ever imagined."

Pantheon with Beam

But, when I hit the ground in Moscufo, my grandfather's hometown, from a departed bus, I felt something different. Time stood still, with a quietness, and I felt their presence, as if they watched from about fifty feet above, hiding behind a cloud. The presence of theirs was palpable. My grandmother, my grandfather and my father, all looking down, as I was walking around, in my grandfather's Italian hometown.

Was there another reason Marco went to Moscufo? The land of his ancestors? It was great to see where his grandfather, Alonso, Sr., had lived as a young boy, til the age of sixteen, before he came to America in 1911.

Just like their presence he felt upon arriving, there was something else he felt alongside that. It was indiscernible at the time, but in retrospect, there was something underneath the surface, on why he longed so much to go there, into the deepest heart of his Italian past.

He first wanted to land, touch and feel that Italian landscape. But, underneath the surface, he went looking for some kind of answer, that maybe the land itself would give him. The land that was tied to his bloodline.

Unconsciously, he was just "listening" on what that Italian air in Moscufo was saying to him that day. Marco went reaching for his Italian past. How he had longed for it so much. Now, he was hungry more than any other time in his life, for all things Italian.

Solo Gondolier on the Walk Home

It was a simple understanding on the surface, but not really simple, how the Italian culture in his life was lost. Twenty years ago, he wasn't even ready to embrace all things Italian. It hurt too much. So, there was much healing that had to be done, from that culture that he, along with his brothers had lost, with the untimely death of their Italian father.

His mother was Irish and so, it would not have been up to her to keep that Italian part of them alive, but she did make a mean spaghetti sauce and her homemade cinnamon rolls from a second generation Irish recipe, were the stuff of legend.

All Those Sundays Ago

They had been cut off from the family, a severing from being part of an Italian clan he used to remember as a kid, going out to his grandma and grandpa's home every Sunday growing up, smelling the sauce cooking as he walked through the door, receiving the multitude of kisses from his aunts, where all the aunts and uncles and cousins would assemble every Sunday, and hearing his grandma and grandpa bark loudly back and forth in Italian. What were they saying? It didn't matter. It was just a beautiful sound, and warm, and we were part of it. The family get togethers, running around in and out of the house, laughing endlessly with his cousins, stealing batches of his aunt's pizzelles, those Italian cookies with the elaborate design, near wafer thin, hundreds it seemed every Sunday, where for many years growing up, us three oldest brothers remember. If we were ever late, we were called by my grandfather Alonso, Sr. and he would say, "Jun! Hurry!" Because dinner was almost ready. My father was Alonso, Jr.

How it all changed. The death of my grandfather in 1965, when I was seven. My mom and dad divorced in 1969, when I was ten. My father had died in 1971, when I was twelve.

They were all we had left in our Italian bloodline and family and our culture, our aunts and uncles and our grandmother. Grandma Gia never changed in her love for us. Nor did some of the aunts and uncles, but that was different than being included as part of the family. How Grandma loved to see us whenever we walked through the door at her new home. She would always yell out our names, when we walked into her kitchen. That was when we went to visit her on our own with our mom, who was welcomed back in by Grandma.

There are reasons I'll never know why we were cut off from the rest of our Italian family, after our father died. Maybe it was hard for them to see us, as it was a reminder of a difficult relationship with our father? Maybe it was my mom divorcing my father that affected my aunts and uncles, that she should have stayed with him, despite my dad becoming physically abusive to my mom, and along with his womanizing and infidelity, she had no choice.

You would have thought with a family of five boys aged fifteen down to the youngest of four years of age, all still kids, that the Italian family we grew up with, at least us older ones remember, that with the horrible loss of our father, that we would have been embraced all the more by our Italian aunts and uncles. Some did for awhile, on and off, but it did not last. The "cut off" could have been unintentional, but there were people in the family that were only ten to fifteen minutes away, that could have cared more than they did. Not long after our father was gone, there was no longer any interest from them, on how we were doing. How their presence in our lives could have made a difference.

There was one relative of my dad's family, my aunt, who lived much farther away, who treated me quite differently. When I left for two years at photography school in Dayton, Ohio, and after all the savings and grants fell short, I was looking at dropping out, before I really got started. This dear aunt and uncle, my dad's sister and her husband, saw to it that I would finish my schooling.

It was not easy to ask for the financial help, and yes, she had the financial resources to help me, but more importantly, she had the heart to care, that I would make it through, so I could be the professional photographer I dreamed of becoming.

"I will never forget your helping me get through photography school, Aunt Rita and Uncle Carl. I couldn't have got my start without your help. Thank you so much."

My grandma had invited my mom back into the fold of the family, on the day of our father's funeral. From then on, we were to be invited back to holiday family functions, and we did go for awhile, for a few years. Until the year we were invited for Christmas dinner at my uncle's home, who was my Italian Godfather, and everyone was there. There was something pivotal that day, that made it hard for my mom to bring us out anymore.

It was on that Christmas, at my uncle's house, and there we were, with the house filled with the family upstairs, my uncle entertaining, playing the piano after dinner, and everyone surrounding him. There we were, in the basement eating our Christmas dinner, alone and cut off from the rest. Not accepted to be part of the gathering upstairs. That said it all, and spoke volumes. No one would come and say, "Come on up here! What are you all doing down there?" We were left to our own space in the basement. I'll never forget that. Alone, like we didn't belong. That was because, in essence, we didn't belong anymore. That was the end of us trying to fit in, at family get togethers, with my father's family.

To the Italian family we grew up with, I will never know how or why this Italian family chose to shun us from being part of the rest of them. They loved when we visited and it was warm and cordial, but we were never made to feel part of the family after our father died. It may have gone back to before my father was gone, on their view of us. It made me feel so unwanted and unaccepted, like tainted goods. We didn't measure up in some way. That loss also included the loss of our Italian culture, that came from family, that no longer wanted us around. My mom never cared that she was ever included, but she cared that her sons were included.

My grandma was very warm toward my mom, welcoming her back into the family, the day of our father's funeral, taking her into her bedroom to telling her, "You were always my daughter-in-law. Not that other one," meaning the second wife my father had married, that later he regretted.

My mom just cared that we were included, but we never were, and that grew over time, into a big hurt. It hurt all my brothers and I. What did we do so wrong to be cut off like this, from what was supposed to be a loving Italian family, the one I knew growing up? Why did they cut us off and not accept us anymore? We were still kids. We didn't know anything, and we had just lost our father.

Our father was stolen from us. My mother raised us five boys alone. It hurt her in a different way, to watch us no longer be accepted by blood. Even if we were invited to my grandmother's house for Christmas dinner, it was like we were not part of them. It was palpable. Then, that day in the basement of my uncle's, my Italian Godfather no less, at that Christmas eating our dinner, apart from the rest of them upstairs, my mom had said, as we sat around her eating on the basement steps, "No more. That's enough." We were clearly separated, not part of the warm gathering upstairs.

The reality was, my brothers and I were swept under the family rug, never to be part of my father's family again.

We were still kids. How it hurt so much. Years later, it would influence me to move away from the dark cloud of pain from my hometown.

It would take years to get over it, or let's say, process it. How do you really get over something like that? Then, for me, years later, after carrying around so much hurt, that I had for so long, and after years of talk therapy…I had to forgive them, for whatever reasons they couldn't let us in as a family anymore. For whatever reasons, we as kids still, were shunned from our Italian family we so much loved, and then, losing our Italian culture that went with it.

So, for the longest time, most of my life, all things Italian hurt too much, because it reminded me of what we lost, our father, our family, our culture. The rest of that family had no idea.

Then, about fifteen years ago, I started to hunger for all things Italian again. After my healing from all the hurt and loss, I was able to embrace it again, that Italian culture on my own, with no connection to my painful severed past.

Did they not see,
Did they not feel,
Did they not care…
How much they were hurting us,
by not accepting us anymore,
by not including us anymore?
We were still kids.
How could this be The Italian Way?

We lost so much family.
We lost so much love.
What would my grandfather think,
the patriarch of our Italian ancestry,
of the five boys who were shunned,
by his Italian family?

Marco was prompted to write about all this after visiting Moscufo, that day in Italy. There had been something more for him there. He had no idea, but he had felt something. The bubbling up came unexpectedly, to look at all that had been locked inside, for decades. Until that one day in Moscufo, when it all came to the surface.

"I had no idea I would encounter the memories so thick, weaved into the scenes I would see, into the photographs I would make. It was bittersweet, as I would remember the depth of how much we as a family lost, my brothers and I. The Italian family we would lose forever."

Marco didn't want to think about this, the loss of his Italian relatives, after all these years. He had put all that behind him. But, this visit to his grandfather's hometown in Italy, was a return to that "Italian air" he remembered as a kid. He had not felt that air, that vibe, in over fifty years. That day in Moscufo, it all came back, the remembrance of all that was once good. The feeling of being part of an Italian family, and its love and togetherness.

Grandma's Back Porch on Sunday

The Irish Saving

One day, many months after returning from Italy, Marco and his younger brother Lorenzo had a serious row, a serious argument. His younger brother couldn't understand how Marco had this fascination and love for Italy, along with the love for his father.

"You're obsessed with Italy!" the younger brother barked. "You weren't raised by Italians. They didn't give a shit about you or us! You were raised by an Irish family. Our father hurt our mother. How can you not see how horrible a person he was?"

"I forgive him. And I have a love for him. It doesn't mean I didn't see his behavior," Marco replied. "What do you want me to do? Hate him like you do? I don't. Until you forgive, you won't understand. It's not fairy-tale viewpoint. It's just forgiveness. Have you forgiven him?"

"Sure I have. But he was a son of a bitch. He beat our mother," the younger brother replied.

"I know. I saw it. It was horrible at the end of their marriage. Our father was troubled and in physical pain everyday. He needed help, that our mother tried to get him, near the end of his life, where they were seeing each other again, right before he died. Had our mother never forgiven our father, she would have never seen him again. But, she chose to forgive, and they became friends like never before."

Years earlier, in the divorce fallout between their mother and father, their mom had lost the custody of the children, her five sons. Then, they had moved from Warren to Niles, into the newer, bigger home with their father and his new wife and her two sons. The year was 1970. It ended up being one, long painful year, for the five brothers, in a strange, new, tense-filled home, where the second wife became the nasty, evil stepmother, on how she treated her kids with love, while the five sons of the father, she treated with judgement, indifference and walk-the-line consequences, including the abuse of his brothers, especially the younger ones.

Marco will never forget the day, he saw from the breezeway, his father's second wife, Ramona, waiting for his younger brother to come home from school. It was report card day.

"As I stood watching from the breezeway window, where our stepmother Ramona was standing just outside the window on the sunken court area near the driveway, my younger brother Dario came home, walking up to her, as she demanded to look at his report card. Right after he handed his report card to Ramona, she took one quick glance at it, and immediately swung back her hand, and swiftly slapped my brother full force across his face, so hard that his glasses went flying off onto the ground. While I watched my brother cry his eyes out, I thought, "This is so unbelievably evil and wrong. How could this be happening?" That was such a heartbreaking, horrible moment to see. His brother had just been diagnosed with epilepsy, and was on medication that made it hard for him to learn at that stage.

That scene summed up perfectly what we were living with; out of control, unpredictable, angered behavior from our father's second wife. But he didn't hit us, she did. He left us alone with a monster.

There were other heartbreaking moments to see and hear, too numerous to mention. Like the time my older brother Gavino had just walked in and seen Ramona slapping the hell out of our youngest brother, Alonso, III. Seeing this, Gavino snapped and punched Ramona in the gut. Then, he climbed out of the upstairs bedroom window onto the roof, and ran down to my Aunt Charlotte's house, a street away, for refuge.

Shortly after, I saw Ramona bring out all my older brother's boxed models into the breezeway, to be thrown into the fireplace. Gavino had been a master model builder at a young age, and our stepmother was set to destroy all his models. Then, twelve year old mousey me said, "You can't do that."

She leaped out like a lion and yelled in my face,"What Do You Mean I Can't Do That! Yes I Can!!"

I thought, "This lady's crazy, and evil."

Our father, was working two jobs, one by day, in a metal fabrication plant, and the other one by night, as a musician drummer. How he didn't see what was really going on in this house, that was not a home, on how the scales were tipped against his sons, from his second wife, while her kids got a free pass everyday. Then, the horrible fighting began between my father and his second wife. Now, she began to receive the beatings.

My father had found out what was really going on when he was away during the day. My two youngest brothers, Lorenzo and Alonso, III, had been getting beat daily. Lorenzo had walked in the upstairs living room one day, and saw our father beating the daylights out of our stepmother Ramona, because he had found out she was beating Lorenzo and Alonso, III, everyday, for wetting the bed as little kids. I think the other part of my father's anger was that he was angry at himself, for choosing this other woman, that he had put his boys through hell with her. How we all wanted to flee, but we were trapped for awhile in a dark place.

The light that would shine during that time, was when our our mother would come to pick us up for our visits with her, where she would take us out to Austintown, Ohio, where she lived with my Irish grandfather who had just lost his wife, our grandmother. Those times were our better days, filled with hope and light, and temporary peace. We would wonder, "How can we get out of where we are, Mom?" Unbeknownst to us at that time, my mom was working behind the scenes with a county prosecutor and my grandfather Bill Shanahan, on getting custody of us back, my brothers and I, where she would succeed in rescuing us.

When my mom's current attorney had failed to help her, this caring county prosecutor Mitchell Shepherd, let my mom know, "If you can get those records from your attorney, I can help you get your kids back." So, my mom and her only sister, my Aunt Charlotte, distracted my mom's attorney's secretary one day and they stole the records out of that office, that she needed, with them running down the street. Later on, with my mom's help, my grandfather secured a new home for us in a good neighborhood, on Bentley Avenue, near a good school, Washington Elementary and Junior High in Niles, Ohio, our hometown. Then, one day she asked us, "Do you want to come live with grandpa and me?" It was a no brainer. I'll never forget it, but it did come bittersweet.

I was the last one to get out of the car that day, when our father dropped us off, seeing him alive for the last time. I wanted both of them, my mom and my dad, but sadly, it couldn't be. My dad then said, "Go on and go." I had felt like I had really let him down, my choosing to go live with my mom and grandpa. It wasn't my fault but I had carried guilt for a few years afterward, until a caring high school teacher helped me get over what I was carrying inside.

My dad was burning the candle at both ends, working two jobs. Factory job by day, professional drummer by night. Even when I was younger, when he and my mom were together, he was always on the go. I wanted to say, "Stay. Please stay."

That year in our new home on Robbins Avenue, with his second wife, we had became a dysfunctional blended family, not due to us. I think he threw the ball with me once. When he would leave that house, from that second marriage, to go drumming at night, I wanted to say, "Stay." Because, he didn't know how unpredictably bad it could get when he left us with her. We were in school most of the time, but evening is when it became needles and pins. I remember hearing my younger brothers cry when they got their beatings. But of course, our stepmother's children were never, ever treated that way.

Then, when he was home in that second house, it could turn violent with our father turning on his second wife, for whatever the reason was. It was hard to listen to or see. I remember staying away from the house, when we could hear them fighting. Sometimes it was dark before I could come back in, when things settled back down.

Then, one day in a moment of tenderness, my father had us gather around him, my brothers and I, in the family room, and I saw he had tears in his eyes, and he said, "I'm going to get you guys out of here." He knew it wasn't good for us, and that he had made a mistake.

Much earlier on, it was a calmer life, with my mom and dad at home, before their divorce, that I can barely remember now. I can even remember watching TV with The Ed Sullivan Show, and the singers my dad loved to watch. We all watched The Beatles first appearance on Ed Sullivan, back at that time in February of 1964.

The father I miss, is the dad I remember in his best moments. His laugh and smile was infectious. My father was troubled, but the good person he had in himself, was later overshadowed by drugs, alcohol and dysfunction. The fact that my mom saw him in his last days before the end of his life, meant that there had been some kind of reconciliation, after all their love and loss with each other. They still loved each other. That is what I like to remember.

The earlier memories were clouded so badly, from the later day ones. I remember my dad's love for the drums and drumming. How he would practice his sticking on the dining room table every night to warm up before going out to play.

Like remembering my dad playing drums in the living room with his musician friends, and maybe an uncle or two, from time to time. How I would come in from playing and hear the music and thought that was pretty normal, but it was really unique, because nobody else around had a father who was a musician. My older brother Gavino got the job of cleaning and polishing my dad's drums. How I wanted to clean and polish his drums too, but I was too young.

I remember other good memories, like how my father took me clear to Youngstown for my birthday, in that last difficult year, looking for a football helmet with the cage facemask. We ended up finding the New York Jets Joe Namath football helmet at Woolworth's at the Eastwood Mall in Niles. I'll never forget that. Or, the time when I was younger in the 60's, when I rode with him for a late evening grocery run to Lawson's, and I saw a Frankenstein model by Revell on the shelf, and he let me buy it.

I had almost forgotten, how in that last year, my dad would call me in to massage his back, about once or twice a week, and he would give me fifty cents to a dollar each time. He told me, "You can make good money doing this someday." He was on pain killers I later found out, for his back, that may have led to his addictions. But, he still made a living as a professional drummer, because he loved playing the drums.

How buried those memories had become, until that one day in Moscufo, Italy, where…

"I felt the goodness of your spirit, overhead in the square, at Piazza Umberto, shortly after I had touched the Italian ground, of grandpa's hometown. That, you were good underneath the suffering and sickness and bad behavior you must have struggled with, that came out in ugly ways."

I guess my trip to Italy was partly designed for me to separate the good memories from the bad, to show there was good to remember about our father.

The memories for me, as this is my story, is that those memories had to be sifted from the latter day ones, and we had to go live with what was a better, healthier place for us, with my mom and grandfather, who had prepared a loving home for us. The Irish, loving home, where we could be kids once again.

That even, after we went to live with my mom and grandfather, only weeks before my father's death, my mom had been seeing my father again, after all the pain she endured from him, she still loved him, they still loved each other, and spent time together, loving each other again. When he had realized his second marriage had failed, he had come back to his first wife, our mom, unbeknownst to us. Years later, after he died, she would then tell us.

A fractured love story? Yes. But, at least they loved each other again, before he passed away, only weeks later.

After that, it was our mom and grandfather of Irish decent, that picked up the pieces of our fractured beginnings, and saw to it that we had a new start, a new life, a new home, while we struggled, my four brothers and I, each in our own way, with the difficult fallout of losing our father. We each had to find our own way.

It would take years to come to terms with this great loss. It would also take years, after much time in talk therapy, to process out of myself, the extra responsibility placed on me at too young an age, to watch out for and care for my brothers, when I wasn't emotionally equipped to do so, where I began to be concerned for everyone in our household, except myself, until I had to realign myself back into the role of son and brother.

No one will ever understand the walk in my shoes, on how not only losing my father, but losing the chance to have my own family, because I was emotionally spent at too young an age. The Irish saving rescuing years of my childhood, was the end of the innocence of my childhood, the end of my being a kid.

The visit to Moscufo, Italy brought back the warm memories of going out to my grandma's and grandpa's, where I was able to just be a kid, with no heavy responsibility. It should have been that way, after my father died, but those Irish saving years, became doubly loaded for me.

Marco had not forgotten how his Irish mom and grandfather provided a great, new home for him and his brothers, after their life's greatest tragedy, the loss of their father, early on in their lives. He just needed a reminder, on how important and loving that new home was.

If it had not been for their mom and all her efforts, her quest and her drive, to get her boys back, for a better life, for a better home, those five boys would not have had the better place to start again, as difficult as that was.

Thanks to our mom, my brothers and I, all got to succeed in our own individual ways. Older brother Gavino became a skilled machinist and carpenter; Dario became a chef and varied handyman, painter; Lorenzo became an executive chef to the Hollywood elite and artisan baker; Alonso, III, became a drug counselor; and I became a career photographer, a writer and kitchen designer.

After the argument that night with Lorenzo, the following morning, on his way to work, what Marco saw in front of him on the road, made him laugh out loud. "You've got to be kidding," he said to himself.

It was a box truck with a big Irish clover on the back door. He immediately took the picture and sent it to his brother. It was a clear reminder of the Irish part of the whole, on how that second stage upbringing played a bigger role. For Marco, it was a loaded launch, that would take years of healing and unraveling, but he was so grateful for the rescuing and raising from the Irish love of his mom and grandpa.

Irish Clover Truck

Doorways

The trip to Italy was a trip through many doorways, to give Marco a sense of how far he had come, from his difficulties throughout the years.

There was the doorway of facing the past, that he had looked at and understood, long before he landed in Rome. Making peace with his Italian past was the impetus that gave him back the love and desire for all things Italian again.

There was the doorway of traveling alone into a foreign land, the fear of navigating alone, on a trip so far from home, that took much courage. He had never known anyone personally that had done that before, like even traveling without some kind of group.

There was the doorway of getting the photographs, one of his main reasons for going. Did he still have what it took, to bring back the goods, the quality of imagery he had dreamed of? Would he be too intimidated in that land by himself, to put the energy and focus into making the images? Not at all. He was always "at home" with himself, whenever he had a camera.

After all, the camera and Marco had been friends to each other since he was sixteen years old. As soon as he got on Italian land, he was off and running. He would just need to know the locations of the key areas he had laid out before he arrived. He had planned it all so well.

Lastly, there was the doorway of being open. Open to surprises, open to unexpected setbacks, like the loss of his cellphone on the first night in Venice, that gave way to the lost zig-zag walk home, from St. Mark's Square to Cannaregio, where he found more beauty in neighborhoods he would have never seen, had it not had been for the new cellphone as a navigational GPS tool, with a British speaking Google lady.

All these doorways allowed him to return home as a new person, where the trip showed, how far he had grown, that had taken many years, decades even, but Marco had learned to trust God in all those onion skin years of healing, that would eventually get him to Italy, that would eventually get him to Moscufo.

Each day, he entered a new doorway, that took him into the deeper part of his trip. Returning home, each day he entered a new doorway of reflection and connection, that gave the trip a deeper ripening of meaning and discovery.

Three Arches at Piazza San Marco, Venice

The Gift of a Lifetime

Some years ago, his love of the camera, and all that it gave him, got disconnected. Too much from life got in the way. Then, the camera, his tool of imaginary delights since high school, began to call on him one day, then on another day, then yet another. Had he forgotten how much he had missed it, that love of the camera and lens that he had known his whole life, better than any single thing else? Still, it would take time, to accept the camera's calling. Did he really want it anymore? Was the passion gone? Or, was it just buried somehow? It would speak to him again, reminding him of his gift, trained and instinctive, how he could work that camera in his hands.

After years of getting reacquainted, he was back with his friend, the camera, that got him through much loss. It helped him forget all the pain, and gave him a new pathway.

Then came Italy. The gifts that came from the trip of a lifetime, were so many, it would take months to fully comprehend everything. How long was the string of miracles, in scenes, experiences and photographs he had captured.

Besides the beautiful photographs he had made, what was it that Marco brought back home from Italy? It would be like returning home in a new skin. The healing, the photographs, and the warm embrace of all things Italian, he now had a great new memory.

That the people and places of Rome, Venice, Pescara and Moscufo, all showed love and acceptance of him, in that foreign land, the land of his ancestors, much more so than some of the Italian people from his own extended family ever did, in his hometown, since his father's passing, all those years ago.

Now, he would have healing icons grace his walls, in the form of all the wonderful photographs he made, to remind himself on how that blessed place shaped like a boot, gave him back his love for all things Italian. How he and that country met each other across the Atlantic, and how he was embraced again, on what it meant to be Italian. How he would never forget, the Pantheon in Rome with its hole in the roof, its sightline to the heavens, touching the four bronze horses galloping at the top of St. Mark's in Venice, and the gondola ride past Marco Polo's house, with the quietness of that gondola boat, in that serene canal. Then, the forty-five minute bus ride out to Moscufo from Pescara, past the olive fields, to where he touched the ground and made the lasting selfie, at the Piazza Umberto, where his grandpa, his grandma and his father, all watched from that cloud, fifty feet above, where Marco had walked. They were happy to see that he had touched ground that day, but they were happier still, that his love for all things Italian had returned to his life, like it had been on all those Sundays ago, when all the plates were filled with pasta, meatballs and sauce, passed around with fresh bread and loving, smiling faces. He had remembered, how it once was being Italian.

Then, in addition to all the amazing things of Italy, the new appreciation came for the Irish part of himself. He remembered how his mom's cinnamon rolls baking, filled the air in the kitchen, all those years ago, where he and his brothers each received their own cinnamon roll pan, where a new home had been made. Thanks to his Irish grandfather and mother, who fought to get them safely into a new home, when he and his brothers needed it most, where they could discover their own hearts and how they could race. The safety and love of that home, allowed Marco to search and discover, the photographer and artist he would become.

Both halves, the Italian and the Irish, would now be integrated. The return of one ancestral culture, and the renewed appreciation of the other, the one that raised him with love.

"I would reach and touch, Italy for myself. It was now mine, all things Italian. In many ways, I got to touch something, reclaim something, bring home something from Italy, that no one in our family has ever seen or touched, or maybe ever will, like I have. More importantly, I became whole again, bringing back home what I had lost, all those years ago. My Italian culture."

Miracles can take a lifetime. The pictures from Italy now adorned his walls, to remind him what he had reached and brought back home, a new place for his heart to beat, from his ancestry, from a place called Italy, where love and healing finally came, from a place called Moscufo.

As they hovered in that cloud that day, from fifty feet above, his grandpa Alonso, his grandma Gia, and his father, Alonso, Jr., whispered and prayed, as they watched him touch the ground that day, while he made that most treasured photograph, at the Piazza Umberto in Moscufo, where those three looking down said, "It's time. Let Marco write it."

And so he did.

The Treasured Touch in Moscufo

About The Author

Mark Toro is a professional photographer and kitchen designer, based in Columbus, Ohio. He began making photographs at age sixteen, photographing classic rock acts in concert like Queen, The Who and Genesis. After winning a few early photography awards, he decided on photography as a career. A graduate of Ohio Institute of Photography, he worked twelve years as a corporate photographer, traveling five states for corporate communications, sometimes on a lear jet. Side projects along the way, allowed him to grow as an artist.

Later, he photographed concerts professionally for publications, covering the top rock acts of the day like, U2, Peter Gabriel, Natalie Merchant and The Rolling Stones. Losing his corporate position to company restructuring, he worked freelance for a few years until he realized he needed to make photographs solely for himself, continuing his professional level, lifetime body of work. His favorite shooting has always been black and white street photography, fashion portraits, and more recently, travel and architectural. While his photography ebbed and flowed over the years, writing became a new passion.

In a chance meeting Al Pacino one night in 1982, in New York City, Mark approached Mr. Pacino with a story idea he had drafted only days earlier for a synopsis "Godfather III." Al had his agent call Mark to see what his story was about. The agent offered an opportunity to have a finished script read, if Mark had one. That profound experience years ago, began Mark's love of writing. His first published piece was a Paul McCartney rock concert review from 1993. Later he dabbled in fiction and published his first novel in 2010.

This particular novel story began unfolding on his first trip to Italy in 2019, while on a train from Venice to his grandfather's hometown region of Pescara. Various life events led up to this journey, but Mark had no idea how vast the effects of his trip would be. In the most mysterious and beautiful way possible, this journey ended up changing his life and healing his past.

Printed in the United States
by Baker & Taylor Publisher Services